CALL to FAITH

W9-CCD-805

GRADE 6
Parish

Harcourt Religion Publishers

www.harcourtreligion.com

The Subcommittee on the Catechism, United States Conference of Catholic Bishops, has found this catechetical series, © 2009 Edition, to be in conformity with the *Catechism of the Catholic Church*.

Nihil Obstat
Rev. Richard L. Schaefer

Imprimatur
✠ Most Rev. Thomas Wenski
Bishop of Orlando
December 14, 2007

The Imprimatur is an official declaration that a book or pamphlet is free of doctrinal or moral error. No implication is contained therein that anyone who granted the Imprimatur agrees with the contents, opinions, or statements expressed.

Copyright © by Harcourt Religion Publishers
2009 Edition

All rights reserved. No part of this publication may be reproduced or transmitted in any form or by any means, electronic or mechanical, including photocopy, recording, or any information storage and retrieval system, without permission in writing from the publisher.

Requests for permission to make copies of any part of the work should be addressed to School Permissions and Copyrights, Harcourt, Inc., 6277 Sea Harbor Drive, Orlando, Florida 32887-6777. Fax: 407-345-2418.

CALL TO FAITH, HARCOURT and the Harcourt Logo are trademarks of Harcourt, Inc., registered in the United States of America and/or other jurisdictions.

For permission to reprint copyrighted material, grateful acknowledgment is made to the following sources:

Confraternity of Christian Doctrine, Washington, D.C.: Scriptures from the *New American Bible*. Text copyright © 1991, 1986, 1970 by the Confraternity of Christian Doctrine. All rights reserved. No part of the *New American Bible* may be used or reproduced in any form, without permission in writing from the copyright owner.

The Estate of Roland F. Palmer: From "Sing of Mary" by Roland F. Palmer. Lyrics © by Estate of Roland F. Palmer.

Henry Holt and Company: "A Time to Talk" from *The Poetry of Robert Frost*, edited by Edward Connery Lathem. Text copyright © 1969 by Henry Holt and Company.

Hope Publishing Co., Carol Stream, IL 60188: Lyrics from "Spirit-Friend" by Tom Colvin. Lyrics © 1969 by Hope Publishing Co. Lyrics from "Sing a New Song to the Lord" by Timothy Dudley-Smith. Lyrics © 1973 by Hope Publishing Co. Lyrics from "Lord, You Give the Great Commission" by Jeffery Rowthorn. Lyrics © 1978 by Hope Publishing Co.

Hyperion: From "When I Die (Part II)" in *Journey Through Heartsongs* by Mattie Stepanek. Text copyright © 2001 by Mattie Stepanek.

International Commission on English in the Liturgy: From the English translation of "The Penitential Rite" and "Renewal of Baptismal Vows" in *Rite of Christian Initiation of Adults*. Translation © 1985 by International Committee on English in the Liturgy, Inc. English translation of "Act of Contrition" from *Rite of Penance*. Translation © 1974 by International Committee on English in the Liturgy, Inc. English translation of "Confiteor" from *The Roman Missal*. Translation © 1973 by International Committee on English in the Liturgy, Inc. English translation of "Prayer After Meals" (Retitled: "Thanksgiving After Meals") from *Book of Blessings*. Translation © 1988 by International Committee on English in the Liturgy, Inc. English translation of Prayer to the Holy Spirit, "Angelus" ("The Angel") and "Memorare" from *A Book of Prayers*. Translation © 1982 by International Committee on English in the Liturgy, Inc. From the English translation of "Eternal Rest" in *Order of Christian Funerals*. Translation © 1985 by International Committee on English in the Liturgy, Inc.

Additional acknowledgments appear on page 278.

Printed in the United States of America

0-15-902279-7   978-0-15-902279-5

If you have received these materials as examination copies free of charge, Harcourt Religion Publishers retains title to the materials and they may not be resold. Resale of examination copies is strictly prohibited and is illegal.

Possession of this publication in print format does not entitle users to convert this publication, or any portion of it, into electronic format.

4 5 6 7 8 9 10 073 12 11 10 09

Grade 6 Contents

© Harcourt Religion

1 God Speaks

■ God reveals himself and his plan of salvation through Scripture.

■ The most important truth of both Sacred Scripture and Tradition is that God is faithful and wants you to live with him forever.

S C R I P T U R E

Ruth and Naomi

Ruth 1:1–17

2 In the Beginning

■ The stories of creation from the Book of Genesis reveal that God alone created the universe.

■ God created man and woman in his own image to live in harmony with him for all eternity.

S C R I P T U R E

First Story of Creation

Genesis 1:1–30

Second Story of Creation

Genesis 2:4–25

3 God's Faithfulness

■ God fully revealed his faithfulness to humans by sending his only Son, Jesus, to conquer sin and bring everlasting life.

■ Humans have the ability to live in friendship with God.

S C R I P T U R E

The First Sin

Genesis 3, 4, 7, 9

The Tower of Babel

Genesis 11:1–9

© Harcourt Religion

© Harcourt Religion

© Harcourt Religion

© Harcourt Religion

Catholic Source Book

Faith in Action: Catholic Social Teaching

© Harcourt Religion

About You

© Harcourt Religion

Let Us Pray

Leader: Help us to love as you love, O Lord.

"Give thanks to the LORD, who is good, whose love endures forever."

Psalm 118:1

All: Help us to love as you love, O Lord. Amen.

Activity Let's Begin

A Journey Year A new year is ahead of you. You can think of the new year as a journey. You will visit Egypt, the ancient land of the pharaohs. You will travel through Palestine, where kings and prophets lived and where Jesus walked the earth. And you will set sail with the Apostles as they proclaim the good news of Jesus to the world.

Your teacher and classmates are on this journey, too. You might not know everyone in your class. Take some time to share something about yourself.

WHAT ARE SOME WORDS THAT DESCRIBE YOU?

About Your Faith

A wonderful world awaits you this year. You will become reacquainted with people from the Bible, and you will have the chance to meet many new ones. You will learn more about God's kingdom and his love for all people. Your family and parish will support you as you discover more about your faith and grow as a member of the Church.

Activity

Share Your Faith

Reflect: What do you know about the kingdom of God? What did Jesus teach about the kingdom?

Share: In small groups share your thoughts.

Act: Describe the kingdom of God in your own words.

_____

_____

_____

SCHOOL BUS

2

© Harcourt Re

About Your Book

The Bible and your *Call to Faith* book are like guides on this journey. Your book includes scripture stories, biographies of saints and stories of real life people, activities, and much more.

Activity

Connect Your Faith

Go on a Scavenger Hunt To get to know your book better, look for the specific features listed below. Write down where you find each of them.

✝ SCRIPTURE   The Washing of the Disciples' Feet _____

BIOGRAPHY   Dorothy Day _____

Words of Faith   **Decalogue** _____

People of Faith   Blessed Peter To Rot _____

Let Us Pray   Prayer of Praise _____

© Harcourt Religion

A Call to Faith

Gather

Pray the Sign of the Cross together.

Leader: Blessed be God.

All: **Blessed be God for ever.**

Leader: Let us pray.

Bow your heads as the leader prays.

All: **Amen.**

Listen to God's Word

Reader: A reading from the holy Gospel according to Luke.

Read Luke 8:1–3.

The Gospel of the Lord.

All: **Praise to you, Lord Jesus Christ.**

Dialogue

Why do you think the women followed Jesus and provided for the group?

How can you provide for the needs of Jesus' followers?

Prayer of the Faithful

Leader: The women of Galilee traveled with Jesus and believed. We ask the Lord to fill us with the courage of these women as we offer our prayers.

Respond to each prayer with these words.

All: **Lord, hear our prayer.**

© Harcourt Religion

Signing of the Senses

Leader: Let us pray.
Jesus, you welcome us into your life.

All: **We want to learn more about you.**

Trace the Sign of the Cross on your forehead.

Leader: Jesus, you ask us to have faith.

All: **We believe in you.**

Trace the Sign of the Cross on your heart.

Leader: Jesus, you call us to help those in need.

All: **We want to bring kind words to all.**

Trace the Sign of the Cross on your mouth.

Go Forth!

Leader: Let us go forth to share our love for Jesus.

All: **Thanks be to God.**

Sing together.

We are called to act with justice,
we are called to love tenderly,
we are called to serve one another;
to walk humbly with God!

"We Are Called" © 1988, 2004 GIA Publications, Inc.

© Harcourt Religion

Prayer and Worship

You can pray to God in many ways. One of the most important ways the Church prays is in the liturgy, or the official public prayer and worship. During the year, members of the Church gather to celebrate different feasts and seasons. These times are marked by the celebration of liturgy. This is why the Church year is called the *liturgical year*.

The seasons and feasts of the liturgical year recall the birth, life, death, Resurrection, and Ascension of Jesus. The liturgical year also honors Mary and the saints. The seasons have colors, symbols, and rituals that help the Church celebrate. These things help us respond to God's life and love.

Symbols and Rituals

The Bible is reverenced by bowing and sitting before it in silence.

The Cross is reverenced by kneeling in front of it or kissing it.

The sign of Christ's peace is offered by a handshake or other gesture.

The Sign of the Cross is marked on foreheads, hearts, and lips.

Holy water is used as a reminder of Baptism.

During the year, your class will use these rituals to celebrate the different seasons.

© Harcourt Religion

The Liturgical Year

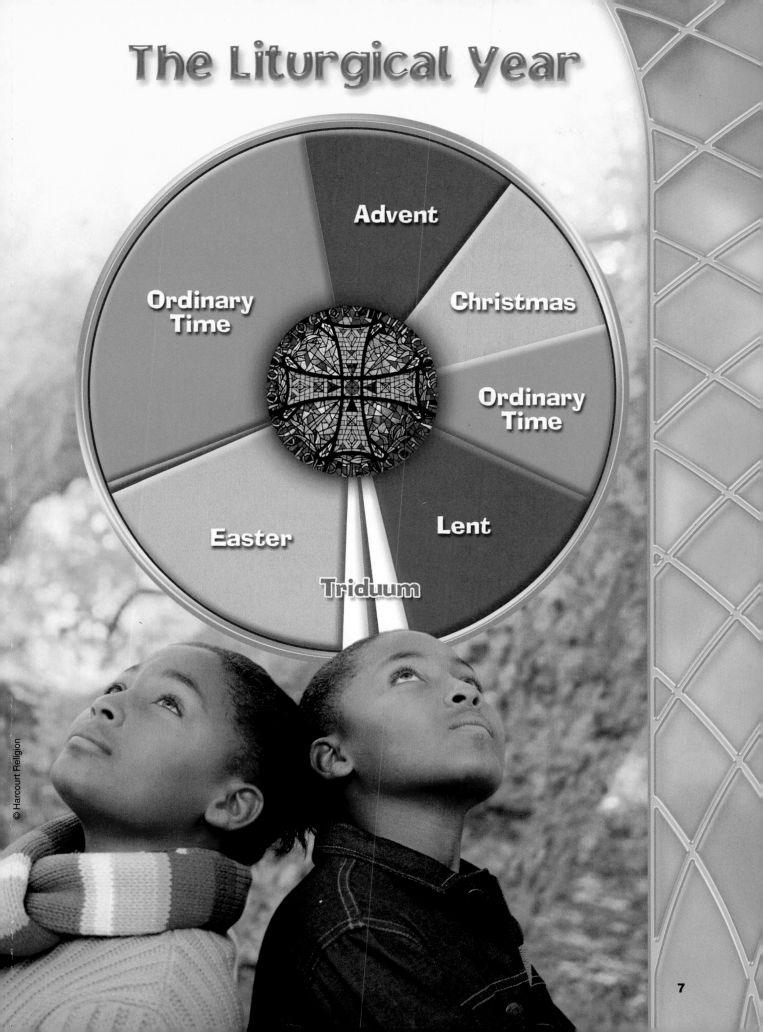

- Advent
- Christmas
- Ordinary Time
- Lent
- Triduum
- Easter
- Ordinary Time

© Harcourt Religion

Presentation of Mary

On November 21 in Ordinary Time, the Church celebrates the feast of the Presentation of the Blessed Virgin Mary. Mary's parents were religious people who practiced the Jewish faith. One Jewish custom was to present a young child in the Temple and dedicate him or her to God's service. According to tradition, Anne and Joachim took Mary to the Temple for this ceremony.

Dedication

Mary has long been honored as a model of faith. We do not know the details of Mary's childhood. But we do know that when she was asked by God to be the mother of his Son, she said "yes." Her *yes* changed the world. Why was Mary so willing to do as God asked? Her dedication to God helped her to do his will. The dedication ceremony in the Temple was just the beginning of her journey of faith. As she grew up, she must have spent much time praying and serving others. This made her dedication to God grow even stronger.

You have been dedicated to God through your Baptism. You, too, are called to a life of prayer and service. Mary's example will help you as you grow in God's friendship and grace.

❓ What has your journey of faith been like? Who has encouraged you to say "yes" to God?

© Harcourt Religion

Celebrate Mary

Gather

Pray the Sign of the Cross together.

Sing together.

Sing of Mary meek and lowly,
Virgin-mother pure and mild,
Sing of God's own Son most holy,
Who became her little child.
Fairest child of fairest mother,
God the Lord who came to earth,
Word made flesh, our very brother,
Takes our nature by his birth.

"Sing of Mary, Meek and Lowly," Roland F. Palmer

Leader: Blessed be God.

All: **Blessed be God for ever.**

Leader: Let us pray.
Bow your heads as the leader prays.

All: **Amen.**

Listen to God's Word

Reverencing Scripture

Leader: Lord, open our minds so that we may understand your word.

All: **Lord, open our hearts so that we may live by your word.**

Stand silently as some class members carry the Bible to the prayer table. When the Bible is placed on its stand, take turns respectfully bowing in front of it.

© Harcourt Religion

Reader: A reading from the prophet Isaiah.
Read Isaiah 61:10–11.
The word of the Lord.

All: **Thanks be to God.**

Dialogue

How does this reading apply to Mary?

Who are some people who are working for justice and praising God?

Intercessions

Leader: Let us pray. Gracious God, you never cease to hear the needs and hopes of your people. With trust we bring our prayers to you now.

Respond to each intercession with these words.

All: **Lord, hear our prayer.**

Leader: Let us pray the words Jesus taught us.

All: **Our Father . . .**

Go Forth!

Leader: Go forth now to dedicate yourself to the word of God and the example of Mary.

All: **Thanks be to God.**

In Dedication

Mary said "yes" to being the Mother of God. God asks you to say *yes* to him in your daily life. He asks you to dedicate yourself to him as Mary did.

❓ **What are some practical ways for you to dedicate yourself to God?**

ACTIVITY

Read the Bible

To learn more about what is written in the Bible about dedication, read one of the following passages on each day of the coming week. Write what meaning you get from each passage.

1. *Song of Songs 8:6–7*
2. *Isaiah 44:1–5*
3. *Colossians 3:1–4*
4. *Acts 4:32–35*
5. *Matthew 11:25–30*
6. *Luke 10:38–42*
7. *John 17:20–26*

© Harcourt Religion

Anticipation

Catholics spend the four weeks before Christmas anticipating and preparing for the coming of Jesus Christ. This season of the liturgical year is called Advent, which means "coming." You get ready to rejoice in the fact that the Son of God became man and was born into the world. But Advent draws your attention to something more. It helps you anticipate and prepare for Jesus' second coming, his return to the world at the end of time.

Second Coming

Jesus told his disciples that there would come a day when "the sun will be darkened, and the moon will not give its light, and the stars will be falling from the sky, and the powers in the heavens will be shaken" (Mark 13:24–25). It is then that Jesus will return in glory. "[He] will send out the angels and gather [his] elect from the four winds, from the end of the earth to the end of the sky" (Mark 13:27).

Jesus' second coming will be the last day of human history. On that day those who have not loved God and neighbor will be forever separated from God's love. Those who have led good lives will be embraced. And all who have died believing in Jesus will rise to greet him. There will come a new heaven and a new earth. All will be well.

❓ **If the second coming happened today, what would Jesus' review of your life be like?**

© Harcourt Religion

Celebrate Advent

Gather

Pray the Sign of the Cross together.

Leader: Our help is in the name of the Lord.

All: **Who made heaven and earth.**

Sing together.

Prepare the way of the Lord.
Prepare the way of the Lord,
and all people will see the salvation of our God.

"Prepare the Way of the Lord" © 1984, Les Presses de Taizé,
GIA Publications, Inc., agent

Leader: Let us pray.
Bow your heads as the leader prays.

All: **Amen.**

Listen to God's Word

Reader 1: A reading from the prophet Isaiah.
Read Isaiah 40:1–5, 9–11.
The word of the Lord.

All: **Thanks be to God.**

*Take a moment of silence to let the word of God speak
to your heart and mind.*

Side 1: I will listen for the word of God;
surely the Lord will proclaim peace.

Side 2: To his people, to the faithful,
to those who trust in him.

Side 1: Near indeed is salvation for the loyal;
prosperity will fill our land.

Side 2: Love and truth will meet;
justice and peace will kiss.

Psalm 85:9–11

© Harcourt Religion

Reader 2:   A reading from the Second Letter of Peter.

Read 2 Peter 3:8–14.

The Word of the Lord.

All: **Thanks be to God.**

Dialogue

What message of hope do you get from these readings?

What can you do to prepare for Jesus' second coming?

Go Forth!

Final Blessing

Bow your heads as the leader prays.

Leader: May the Lord bless us and keep us.

All: **Amen.**

Leader: May the Lord's face shine upon us.

All: **Amen.**

Leader: May the Lord look upon us with kindness, and give us peace.

All: **Amen.**

GIA Publications, Inc.

Leader: Go forth and prepare a place for Jesus in your heart and make ready for his second coming.

All: **Thanks be to God.**

© Harcourt Religion

Prepare for Jesus' Coming

During Advent the Church directs your attention to the birth of Jesus in the past, his second coming in the future, and his presence with you now. As you prepare to celebrate the joyful feast of Christmas, prepare yourself also to be ready for Jesus' return in glory at the end of time. No one knows when this will happen. The second coming could be tomorrow, or it could be thousands of years from now.

❓ **What are some things you can do in your everyday life to prepare for the coming of the Lord?**

Sunday	Monday	Tuesday	Wednesday	Thursday	Friday	Saturday
		1	2	3	4	5

(ACTIVITY)
At the Center

The Season of Advent reminds you to make Jesus the center of your life. With a partner discuss things you can do to make Jesus the most important part of your daily living. Share your ideas with the class. Choose one thing to do for each week of Advent.

© Harcourt Religion

Season of Peace

As the Jewish people waited for the Messiah, they heard many prophecies. They learned that a virgin would give birth to a son and call him Immanuel. He would be known as "Wonder-Counselor, God-Hero, Father-Forever, Prince of Peace" (*Isaiah 9:5*). The reign of this child would be vast and forever peaceful. (*See Isaiah 9:6*). Christmas celebrates the arrival of this long awaited Prince of Peace.

Prince of Peace

When Jesus was born, the heavenly host praised God and proclaimed to the shepherds, "Glory to God in the highest and on earth peace to those on whom his favor rests" (*Luke 2:14*). After his Resurrection Jesus greeted people with the words "Peace be with you" (*John 20:19*).

The peace Jesus offers is rooted in the promise that no matter what happens to you, God is with you. You can be confident that God's loving presence is with you every minute of the day. With this confidence comes a deep sense of peacefulness.

A wonderful way to celebrate Jesus' birth is to commit yourself to peacemaking. You promote peace by respecting others and recognizing the dignity of all people. You become a peacemaker by praying for peace and asking God to end conflicts between neighbors and nations. And you make the world more peaceful by working for justice in your home, school, and community.

 Who are peacemakers in your home and school? How can you be a peacemaker?

© Harcourt Religion

Celebrate Peace

Gather

Sing together.

Peace before us, peace behind us, peace
  under our feet.
Peace within us, peace over us, let all around
  us be peace.

Love before us, love behind us, love under
  our feet.
Love within us, love over us, let all around
  us be love.

"Prayer of Peace," David Haas © 1987, GIA Publications, Inc.

Pray the Sign of the Cross together.

Leader:	Blessed be the name of the Lord.
All:	**Now and for ever.**
Leader:	Let us pray.
	Bow your heads in silent prayer. Then listen as the leader prays.
All:	**Amen.**

Listen to God's Word

Reader:	A reading from the holy Gospel according to Luke.
	Read Luke 2:8–14.
	The Gospel of the Lord.
All:	**Praise to you, Lord Jesus Christ.**

Spend a few moments in silence thinking about the words of God.

© Harcourt Religion

Intercessions

Leader: Let us pray for the Church and the world, that all will be open to the power of the Holy Spirit.

Respond to each intercession with these words.

All: **God, bring us your peace.**

Our Father and Sign of Peace

Leader: Let us call on our Loving Father as Jesus taught us.

All: **Our Father . . .**

Leader: Our Lord Jesus offers you peace. Pray for the peace and unity of his kingdom now and forever.

All: **Amen.**

Leader: Let us offer each other a sign of peace.

Turn to your classmates and offer them a handshake or another sign of peace. Remind yourself that as peacemaker, you are giving and receiving a sign of forgiveness and a wish for peace.

Go Forth!

Leader: Go forth in peace. May the love and kindness of Jesus be with you as you share his peace with everyone you meet.

All: **Amen.**

© Harcourt Religion

Let There Be Peace

Peace begins with you. If all people were to do something on a regular basis to bring about peace in their hearts or homes or communities, the world would become a place of peace. There would be less violence, less bullying and selfishness, and less hatred.

? **What do peacemakers do? What is a situation in the world today that needs the skills of a peacemaker?**

ACTIVITY
Peace Poster

As a class, discuss ways to work for peace at school, in your neighborhood, and in the world.

- Consider the situation, what people are doing to help, and other things that can be done.
- Cut headlines and pictures from newspapers and magazines that show people in need of peace and people working for peace.
- Use the clippings to make a Peace Poster. Include your suggestions for making peace a reality.

© Harcourt Religion

Called to Love

During Ordinary Time, the Church celebrates the feasts of many saints. The Church celebrates the life of Saint John Bosco on January 31. Saint John Bosco understood the Christian message of love. He recognized Jesus in each person he served.

Saint John Bosco

Francis and Margaret Bosco lived in Italy in the early nineteenth century. They had three sons, one of whom was John. When John was two years old, his father died. Margaret kept their small farm running with the help of her sons, but the family lived in poverty.

John was a special child. He was very bright and learned how to read and write at a very early age. He also had a wonderful way with the other children. They saw John as a leader, and he helped them settle arguments peacefully.

As John grew up, he heard the call of God to become a priest. John knew that God wanted him to work with children, especially with boys who were orphans or who were in trouble. Before long, Don Bosco, as he was known, began a trade school and an orphanage for boys. The boys learned about their faith and how to live productive lives.

Don Bosco also believed that God was asking him to form a community of priests and brothers. Don Bosco founded the Order of Saint Francis de Sales, or the Salesians. A group of Salesian sisters were also founded. Today the Salesians continue Saint John Bosco's work with young people throughout the world.

? **How did John help young children? What can you do to help?**

© Harcourt Religion

Celebrate Service

Gather

Pray the Sign of the Cross together.

Leader: Our help is in the name of the Lord.

All: **Who made heaven and earth.**

Sing together.

Guide my feet while I run this race.
Guide my feet while I run this race.
Guide my feet while I run this race,
For I don't want to run this race in vain.

Verse 2: I'm your child . . . .
Verse 3: Hold my hand . . . .
Verse 4: Stand by me . . . .

"Guide My Feet," African-American Traditional

Leader: Let us pray.
Bow your heads as the leader prays.

All: **Amen.**

Listen to God's Word

Reader: A reading from the holy Gospel according to John.
Read John 13:33–35.
The word of the Lord.

All: **Praise to you, Lord Jesus Christ.**

© Harcourt Religion

Dialogue

Who has been a wise and loving teacher to you?

How can young people follow the example of Saint John Bosco?

Take a few moments of silence to listen to God speaking to you in the quiet of your heart.

Intercessions

Leader: Let us pray. God our Father, you give us what we need even before we ask. Hear our prayers.

Respond to each intercession with these words.

All: **Lord, hear our prayer.**

Signing of the Senses

Step forward one by one as the leader signs your eyes, lips, and hands with the cross of salvation. After each person is signed, say the following.

All: **Christ will be your strength!**
Learn to know and follow him!

GIA Publications, Inc.

Go Forth!

Leader: Let us go forth this week to love and serve Jesus in all those we meet.

All: **Thanks be to God.**

© Harcourt Religion

Christian Love

Many people do loving things for others. But what makes the loving actions of Christians different? Christians treat others with love and kindness because they believe that what they do for others, they are really doing for Jesus.

? How did John Bosco know what God wanted him to do with his life? What made John Bosco's love for others special?

ACTIVITY
Use Your Talents

What do you enjoy doing? What talents and gifts has God given you? What two talents will you share with others this week? In small groups, talk about how you will share your talents. If possible, share your talents with other children.

Lenten Preparation

The forty days of Lent are a time to reflect on the sufferings and death of Jesus. Lent is also a time to prepare to celebrate Jesus' Resurrection on Easter Sunday. Members of the Church dedicate more time to prayer. They perform works of penance, such as fasting and participating in the Sacrament of Reconciliation. And they make a greater effort to be generous to people who are poor or in need.

Scrutinies

During Lent, those who will receive the Sacraments of Initiation, the elect, enter a time of deep reflection. This period is a time for the elect to deepen their commitment to follow Christ. To help bring about this process, the Church celebrates rituals called scrutinies. There are scrutinies on the Third, Fourth, and Fifth Sundays of Lent.

During the scrutinies, the elect come forward at Mass. The priest greets them and asks them to kneel. He lays his hands on their heads and prays that God will heal and strengthen them. The community prays with the priest and asks God to protect the elect from evil. The community also asks Jesus to give strength and faith to all his followers.

As the elect prepare for Baptism, Confirmation, and the Eucharist, the entire community is renewed.

 How do you think the elect feel as they prepare for the sacraments?

© Harcourt Religion

Celebrate Lent

Gather

Pray the Sign of the Cross together.

Leader: O Lord, open my lips.

All: **That my mouth shall proclaim your praise.**

Sing together the refrain.

Return to God with all your heart,
the source of grace and mercy;
come seek the tender faithfulness of God.

"Return to God," Marty Haugen © 1990, 1991, GIA Publications, Inc.

Leader: Lord,
grant us your pardon and peace,
so that, cleansed of our sins,
we may serve you with untroubled hearts.

We ask this through Christ our Lord.

All: **Amen.**

Listen to God's Word

Reader: A reading from the holy Gospel according
to Luke.

Read Luke 15:1–7.

The Gospel of the Lord.

All: **Praise to you, Lord Jesus Christ.**

Dialogue

When have you felt like the lost sheep? Who has helped
you find your way?

When have you helped others find their way back to God?

© Harcourt Religion

Intercessions

Leader: Let us ask God to make us strong and faithful followers of Jesus.

Lord God, protect us from the evils in the world.

All: **Lord, hear our prayer.**

Leader: Lord God, do not let us be tempted to stray.

All: **Lord, hear our prayer.**

Leader: For what else shall we pray?

After each intercession, all respond:

All: **Lord, hear our prayer.**

Leader: Let us gather all of these things that we want to ask of God into a single prayer.

All: **Our Father . . .**

Penitential Rite

Kneel silently as the leader prays.

Leader: Loving Father,
free these young people from whatever could make them turn from you and help them to walk in your light.

All: **We want to walk with Jesus,**
who gave his life for us.
Help us, Father, to follow him.

From the Penitential Rite, RCIA.

Go Forth!

Leader: Let us go forth this week to share Christ's light and peace with those around us.

All: **Thanks be to God.**

© Harcourt Religion

We Pray, O Lord

Prayer is an important part of Lent. You pray for faith that you may truly appreciate the wonderful gift of life that Easter brings. You pray for hope that you will not let your problems or fears overwhelm you. You pray for charity that you have the generosity to help others in need. And you pray for others, including those in your parish preparing for Baptism, asking God to bless them and keep them safe from all harm.

❓ **How can you make prayer a priority during Lent?**

ACTIVITY
Becoming Members

Find out the names of the people in your parish who will join the Church this Easter. Write a note to one of them, telling that person that you will pray for him or her in a special way on the scrutiny Sundays.

Harcourt Religion

Story of Salvation

The last three days of Holy Week are called the Triduum, a word that means "a period of three days." During this time the Church celebrates the Evening Mass of the Lord's Supper on Holy Thursday, the Lord's Passion on Good Friday, the Easter Vigil on the night of Holy Saturday, and Easter Sunday Mass and Evening Prayer. During these three days the entire story of salvation is proclaimed and celebrated in the liturgy.

From Life to Death

In the opening chapters of the Bible, stories are told to explore the beginning of the human race and the origin of sin. In the stories, God creates the first man and woman to live in friendship with him forever. Adam and Eve choose instead to violate God's friendship and follow their own path. By doing this, they lose paradise and the original holiness God shared with them. Death replaces eternal life as the destiny of humans.

However, God acts in human history to bring his people back to himself. This is seen in key biblical events: God's promise to Abraham, Sarah, and all of Israel, the freeing of the Israelites from slavery, the covenant God made with Moses, the entry into the promised land, the establishment of the kingdom under David, and the bold words of the prophets.

The story of salvation in the Old Testament reaches its fulfillment in the New Testament. The history of salvation is fulfilled in Jesus. The stories and events come together in the life of Jesus. The Triduum celebrates the whole of salvation history that culminates in the Paschal mystery.

 What are some New Testament accounts that show Jesus brings salvation?

© Harcourt Religion

Celebrate Triduum

Gather

Pray the Sign of the Cross together.

Leader: God, come to my assistance.

All: **Lord, make haste to help me.**

Leader: Glory to the Father, and to the Son, and to the
Holy Spirit:

All: **as it was in the beginning, is now, and will be
for ever. Amen.**

Leader: Let us pray.
Bow your heads as the leader prays.

All: **Amen.**

Sing together the refrain.

We hold the death of the Lord deep in our hearts.
Living; now we remain with Jesus the Christ.

"Now We Remain," David Haas © 1983, GIA Publications, Inc.

Listen to God's Word

Reader: A reading from the Letter of Paul to the Romans.
Read Romans 6:3–11.
The word of the Lord.

All: Thanks be to God.

Take a few moments of silence to meditate on the word of God.

Dialogue

How do you participate in Jesus' Passion, death,
and Resurrection?

What are some ways that you can "live for God in
Christ Jesus"?

© Harcourt Religion

Renewal of Baptismal Vows

Leader: During the Easter Vigil liturgy, members of the Church renew their baptismal vows as we will do now.

To each of the following, respond: I do.

Leader: Do you reject sin so as to live in the freedom of God's children?

Do you reject the glamor of evil and refuse to be mastered by sin?

Do you reject Satan, father of sin and prince of darkness?

Do you believe in God, the Father almighty, creator of heaven and earth?

Do you believe in Jesus Christ, his only Son, our Lord, who was born of the Virgin Mary, was crucified, died, and was buried, rose from the dead, and is now seated at the right hand of the Father?

Do you believe in the Holy Spirit, the holy Catholic Church, the communion of saints, the forgiveness of sins, the resurrection of the body, and life everlasting?

RCIA 238–239

Leader: Let us pray.

Bow your heads as the leader prays.

All: **Amen.**

Go Forth!

Leader: Go forth and live the baptismal promises you have renewed.

All: **Thanks be to God.**

© Harcourt Religion

Salvation in Christ

The three days of the Easter Triduum summarize and fulfill the Old Testament's story of salvation. By participating in the liturgies on the three most holy days, you are celebrating your own salvation and that of all who live in Christ.

❓ **What does salvation mean to you?**

© Harcourt Religion

ACTIVITY
The Three Days

Tell one thing you will do on Holy Thursday, Good Friday, and Holy Saturday to show you are a follower of Jesus.

Witnesses

Easter is the feast of the Resurrection of Jesus. It is the oldest and most important celebration in the Church's calendar. Since about the year 300, the Church has celebrated Easter on the first Sunday following the full moon after the spring equinox, between March 22 and April 25. The Easter Season starts on Easter Sunday and continues until Pentecost, fifty days later.

Sharing the Message

Three days after his death, Jesus rose from the dead. Some faithful women had gone to the tomb, but he was not there. He then appeared to them, saying, "Do not be afraid. Go tell my brothers to go to Galilee, and there they will see me" (*Matthew 28:10*). The Gospel according to John tells us that Jesus first appeared to Mary Magdalene.

The glorified Jesus also appeared to the disciples on the road to Emmaus and to the eleven Apostles and other followers.

The disciples and Apostles who saw the glorified Christ became his witnesses. They spread the news around the world just as Jesus told them to do. (*See Acts 1:8.*) By gathering to celebrate the Easter message, you are a witness of Jesus' Resurrection today.

❓ **How does your parish celebrate Easter?**

Celebrate Easter

Gather

♪♪♪♪

Sing together.

Jubilate Deo omnis terra.
Servite Domino in laetitia.
Alleluia, alleluia, in laetitia!
Alleluia, alleluia, in laetitia!

Raise a song of gladness, peoples of the earth.
Christ has come, bringing peace, joy to
ev'ry heart.
Alleluia, alleluia, joy to ev'ry heart!
Alleluia, alleluia, joy to ev'ry heart!

"Jubilate Servite/Raise a Song of Gladness" © 1979,
Les Presses de Taizé, GIA Publications, Inc., agent

Pray the Sign of the Cross together.

Leader: Light and peace in Jesus Christ our Lord, alleluia.

All: **Thanks be to God, alleluia.**

Leader: Let us pray.
Bow your heads as the leader prays.

All: **Amen.**

Listen to God's Word

Leader: A reading from the holy Gospel according
to John.
Read John 20:1–9.
The Gospel of the Lord.

All: **Praise to you, Lord Jesus Christ.**

*Take a few moments to consider how you might place yourself
in the gospel story.*

Dialogue

Where did you place yourself in the gospel story? What did you see or hear there?

Why is Jesus' Resurrection so important?

Presentation of Names

Leader: One way to give witness to your faith in the Resurrection is to commend those who have died to the mercy of God. Take a few minutes to write the names of people who have died whom you wish to remember in prayer. After you have written your list of names, please come forward and place the list in the bowl in the front of the room.

After the last student has come forward, the intercessions begin. Respond to each intercession with these words.

All: **I place my trust and hope in God.**

Go Forth!

Leader: Go forth and live the hope that comes from the Risen Jesus, alleluia, alleluia.

All: **Thanks be to God, alleluia, alleluia.**

© Harcourt Religion

He Is Risen!

Jesus truly was raised from the dead. This event has been the central truth of the Church's faith. From this truth come two other truths: Jesus conquered death so that death has no more power over you, and Jesus gives life to those who have died in him.

? How does the Resurrection of Jesus influence your faith? Your decisions?

ACTIVITY

Scripture Passages

During this coming week, take time to learn more about the Resurrection by reading a passage from Scripture that talks about the Resurrection. Below are seven passages. Read one each day this week. Write down a meaningful word or passage that you will try to remember and live.

1. Matthew 28:1–10
2. Luke 24:13–35
3. John 20:11–18
4. John 20:19–29
5. Acts 10:34–43
6. Acts 13:28–33
7. 1 Corinthians 5:6–8

The Holy Spirit

Fifty days after Easter, the Church celebrates Pentecost Sunday. It is a celebration of the birth of the Church. On Pentecost the Apostles began the work of the Church when the Holy Spirit descended upon them. Through the power of the Holy Spirit, the Apostles began gathering new members into their community.

Gifts of the Spirit

The feast of Pentecost reminds you that, like the Apostles, you have received gifts from the Holy Spirit in Baptism. These gifts are lasting qualities that help you grow in your spiritual and moral life.

Wisdom helps you recognize and do God's will more perfectly. *Understanding* helps you separate what is true from what is false. *Counsel,* also known as right judgment, is the gift of helping others seek the will of God. *Fortitude,* also called courage or strength, gives you the spiritual and moral strength to stand up for what is right. *Knowledge* means knowing the ways of God. *Piety,* also called reverence, helps you focus on God and remain true to your responsibilities. *Fear of the Lord* is awe of God that leads you to give him respect because he is the Creator of all.

As you use the gifts of the Holy Spirit, you become more open to the presence of the Holy Spirit in your life.

❓ **What are some ways you have seen others live out the gifts of the Holy Spirit?**

© Harcourt Religion

Celebrate the Holy Spirit

Gather

Sing together the refrain.

Come, Lord Jesus, send us your Spirit,
renew the face of the earth.
Come, Lord Jesus, send us your Spirit,
renew the face of the earth.

"Send Us Your Spirit," © 1987, David Haas © 1981, 1982, 1987,
GIA Publications, Inc.

Pray the Sign of the Cross together.

Leader: Light and peace in Jesus Christ our Lord, alleluia.

All: **Thanks be to God, alleluia.**

Leader: Let us pray.
Bow your heads as the leader prays.

All: **Amen.**

Listen to God's Word

Reader: A reading from the Acts of the Apostles.
Read Acts 2:1–11.
The word of the Lord.

All: **Thanks be to God.**

*Take a moment of silence to listen for the Spirit in the
word of God.*

Dialogue

How do you think the Apostles felt on Pentecost?

What examples can you find to illustrate the gifts of the Holy
Spirit alive in the Church today?

Choosing a Gift

Respond to each intercession with these words.

All: **Come, Holy Spirit, lead us in the way of Jesus.**

Leader: Holy Spirit, let the way of Jesus be our joy and join us on every step of our journey.

                 Holy Spirit, may we be like trees planted near streams and grow strong in faith, nourished by your life-giving gifts.

                 Holy Spirit, help us always remember that the Father watches over us as we follow the path of his Son.

Leader: Pray now for the gift of the Holy Spirit that you think is most important and necessary for your journey today. Then, walk up to the prayer table and choose the gift for which you prayed.

As you proceed to the prayer table, sing "Send Us Your Spirit."

Leader: Let us pray the prayer that Jesus taught us.

All: **Our Father . . .**

Go Forth!

Leader: Go forth with the confidence that the Holy Spirit is with you and is giving you all that you need to walk the path of faith.

All: **Thanks be to God.**

© Harcourt Religion

Led by the Spirit

Those who are led by the Holy Spirit show the fruits of the Spirit in their lives. For each of the traditional fruits of the Spirit listed below, write one way you show that quality in your words and actions. During this coming week, take time to complete this chart carefully and prayerfully.

ACTIVITY

Fruits of the Spirit	How it is shown in my words and actions
Charity	
Joy	
Peace	
Patience	
Kindness	
Goodness	
Generosity	
Gentleness	
Faithfulness	
Modesty	
Self-control	
Chastity	

© Harcourt Religion

Unit 1
Revelation

In this unit you will...

learn that we come to know what God is like from both Scripture and Tradition. In both, God reveals himself and his desire for us to live in friendship with him. Through the accounts of creation and the establishment of the covenant, we learn that God is faithful. By sending his Son, Jesus, God the Father reveals himself to us in ways we never would have known.

Chapter **1**

Chapter **2**

Chapter **3**

 What do you think you will learn in this unit about God and his faithfulness

© Harcourt Religion

Chapter 1 God Speaks

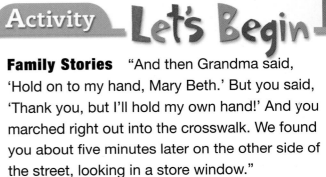

Let Us Pray

Leader: God our Father, thank you for telling us about yourself.

"The revelation of your words sheds light,
gives understanding to the simple."

Psalm 119:130

All: God our Father, thank you for telling us about yourself. Amen.

Activity — Let's Begin

Family Stories "And then Grandma said, 'Hold on to my hand, Mary Beth.' But you said, 'Thank you, but I'll hold my own hand!' And you marched right out into the crosswalk. We found you about five minutes later on the other side of the street, looking in a store window."

The whole family laughed as Mary Beth's mom delivered the familiar punch line. This story was told often at holidays and family reunions.

• Discuss some favorite family stories. Share why you think that certain stories become favorites.

© Harcourt Religion

Storytelling and God's Plan

◎ Focus How do we learn about God and his plan?

Stories help families remember what binds them together. Stories can do the same thing for communities and nations. April is a Native American girl who lives with her grandparents in a pueblo near Santa Fe, New Mexico. Her grandparents are introducing April to the traditions of the Navajo people.

A STORY

THE STORYTELLER

April loved to hear the stories that her grandparents told about the Navajo people. From these colorful tales, she gained knowledge about her roots, respect for all creation, and wisdom for living. Today her grandmother was going to teach her something unique about her people!

Grandmother said, "Our people have always loved stories. They show this by making storyteller figures. Let's make one out of clay."

Grandmother continued, "The main figure of the Storyteller is that of a woman. Her mouth is open because she is speaking, and her eyes may be closed as if she is remembering experiences from an earlier time. Attached to the woman are many children. Crowding around the Storyteller, they listen to the stories of their people's history and of the wonders of creation."

April and her grandmother spent the afternoon working with the clay while April learned more about her family's history. She hoped that someday she would have a chance to retell the same stories to her grandchildren.

❓ Why is it important for a family or a nation to remember its stories?

© Harcourt Religion

Stories About God's Plan

Your community of faith has stories of its own, too. The stories of your faith are told in the Bible and continued in the Tradition of the Church.

The Bible, or Sacred Scripture, is God's word, written by humans acting under God's direction and guidance. The Bible and Tradition together are the source of God's **revelation**, or communication about himself. God, the principal author of the Bible, inspired its human authors. By words and actions, God has made himself known gradually and in stages. This means that God gave the Scripture writers the gift of the Holy Spirit to write faithfully about his saving truth.

The Holy Spirit continues to guide the Church, which preserves and teaches God's revelation. The Church interprets the message of the Bible for each new age through its Tradition so that all can know and apply God's wisdom to their lives.

❓ **What is your favorite story of faith?**

A Community of Storytellers

Many of the stories in the Bible were passed down orally from generation to generation before they were written. Over a period of more than six centuries, various people wrote the books of the Bible.

The Bible presents the story of God's presence and of his saving plan and actions for his people. After many centuries, God fully revealed his plan of **salvation** by sending his Son, Jesus, and then, by sending the Holy Spirit through Jesus.

Words of Faith

Revelation is the process by which God makes himself known. The chief sources of revelation are Scripture and Tradition.

Salvation is the loving action of God's forgiveness of sins and the restoration of friendship with him brought by Jesus.

Activity — Share Your Faith

Reflect: Think about some of your favorite Bible stories.

Share: Share a story with a partner. Explain why it is your favorite.

Act: Write down two things the story tells you about God.

_____

_____

© Harcourt Religion

43

Different Types of Writing in the Bible

 **Focus** What are some of the literary forms used in the Bible?

The Bible writers used different literary forms, or styles of writing, to tell their stories. Some writers composed poems, and some wrote historical accounts. Others recorded wise sayings or messages from God that had been spoken by the prophets. Here are some of the different kinds of writing found in the Bible.

? **Which of these literary forms do you like to read? Why?**

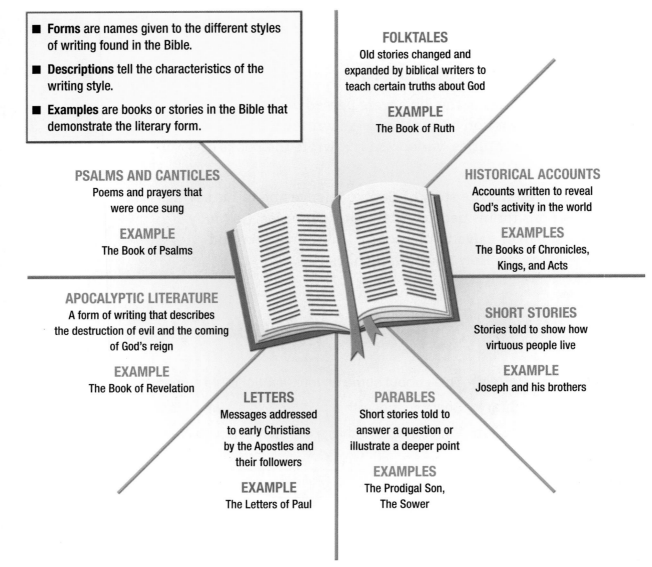

- **Forms** are names given to the different styles of writing found in the Bible.
- **Descriptions** tell the characteristics of the writing style.
- **Examples** are books or stories in the Bible that demonstrate the literary form.

FOLKTALES
Old stories changed and expanded by biblical writers to teach certain truths about God

EXAMPLE
The Book of Ruth

PSALMS AND CANTICLES
Poems and prayers that were once sung

EXAMPLE
The Book of Psalms

HISTORICAL ACCOUNTS
Accounts written to reveal God's activity in the world

EXAMPLES
The Books of Chronicles, Kings, and Acts

APOCALYPTIC LITERATURE
A form of writing that describes the destruction of evil and the coming of God's reign

EXAMPLE
The Book of Revelation

SHORT STORIES
Stories told to show how virtuous people live

EXAMPLE
Joseph and his brothers

LETTERS
Messages addressed to early Christians by the Apostles and their followers

EXAMPLE
The Letters of Paul

PARABLES
Short stories told to answer a question or illustrate a deeper point

EXAMPLES
The Prodigal Son, The Sower

© Harcourt Religion

God's Message

God speaks through all of the literary forms of the Bible. The most important truth of both Sacred Scripture and Tradition is that God is faithful and wants you to live with him forever. Scripture and Tradition contain the truths that guide your life. The story below can be considered a folktale about one woman's coming to believe in God.

Faith Fact

Naomi's name, which means "pleasant," is a sign of God's favor toward her.

✝ SCRIPTURE   The Book of Ruth

Ruth and Naomi

Naomi and her husband left the land of Judah and settled in Moab. Their two sons married women from Moab. Eventually, Naomi's husband and sons died. So she decided to return to Judah.

Her daughters-in-law, Ruth and Orpah, wanted to go with her, but Naomi told them, "Go back to your own homes. May the Lord be as kind to you as you have been to me." Orpah went to her home, but Ruth remained.

Ruth said to Naomi, "Do not ask me to abandon or forsake you! for wherever you go I will go, wherever you lodge I will lodge, your people shall be my people, and your God my God."

Based on Ruth 1:1–17

❓ **What does Ruth's decision to remain with Naomi teach you?**

Activity   Connect Your Faith

Learn About God   Read the passages below. What is the literary form of each passage? What word is God speaking to you in each passage?

Exodus 19:1–7   *Luke 12:16–21*   *Revelation 11:15–19*

© Harcourt Religion

Prayer to the Holy Spirit

Let Us Pray

Gather and begin with the Sign of the Cross.

Leader: The Lord be with you.

All: **And also with you.**

Leader: God our Father, you teach us about yourself in the Bible. Thank you for the Holy Spirit, who guides us in our reading. Help us be like your Son, who makes your word come alive.

Reader: *Read John 14:15–17.*

Leader: Jesus said, ". . . it is better for you that I go. For if I do not go, the Advocate will not come to you. But if I go, I will send him to you."

All: **Come, Holy Spirit, and lead us to God.**

Leader: Jesus said, "I have much more to tell you, but you cannot bear it now."

All: **Come, Holy Spirit, and lead us to God.**

Leader: Jesus said, "But when he comes, the Spirit of truth, he will guide you to all truth."

All: **God our Father, as we learn more about the story of our faith in the Bible, send your Spirit to help us see your loving hand guiding us closer to you. Amen.**

Based on *John 16:7, 12, 13*

Sing together.

Spirit of our Maker,
    Spirit-Friend.
Spirit of our Jesu,
    Spirit-Friend.
Spirit of God's people,
    Spirit-Friend.

"Spirit-Friend", Tom Colvin,
© 1969, 1987 Hope Publishing Co.

© Harcourt Religion

A **Work with Words**   Circle True if a statement is true and circle False if a statement is false. Correct any false statements.

1. The process by which God makes himself known to people in Scripture and Tradition is called revelation.

   True   False   _____

2. The story of God's saving action is found in the Bible.

   True   False   _____

3. Scripture was first passed down in writing.

   True   False   _____

4. News reports are a form of storytelling in the Bible.

   True   False   _____

5. The Holy Spirit helps you open your mind and heart so that you can live the truths of the Bible and Tradition.

   True   False   _____

B **Check Understanding**   What are some ways in which God reveals himself?

_____

Activity   Live Your Faith

Share Stories   The story of Ruth and Naomi teaches a lesson about a woman who comes to believe in God. What is a story of today that could teach a similar lesson? Sketch the main ideas for your story in the three frames. Choose a group to help you, and act out the story for your class.

© Harcourt Religion

Family Faith

Catholics Believe

- God reveals himself and his plan of salvation through Scripture.

- The most important truth of both Sacred Scripture and Tradition is that God is faithful and wants you to live with him forever.

✝ SCRIPTURE

Read *Luke 14:7–14* to learn how you can treat others with loving goodness.

GO ONLINE www.harcourtreligion.com
For weekly Scripture readings and seasonal resources

Activity

Live Your Faith

Write Your Story Just as each person has his or her own story, each family has its own story. Together, write your family story. Include any family history, special memories, or other features that make your family unique. After you have written your story, talk about the ways your family story fits into God's great story of loving goodness.

People of Faith

▲ Saint Hilda of Whitby 614–680

Hilda of Whitby was a princess who lived in England. She gave up the privileges of royalty to devote herself to a life of holiness. Deeply inspired by the Holy Spirit and God's word, she entered religious life. She later founded and presided over the double monastery at Whitby. Because Hilda believed in the value of education, she promoted the reading and study of Scripture in her monasteries, as well as the study of the Latin language and literature. Saint Hilda's feast day is November 17.

Family Prayer

Saint Hilda, pray for us that we may follow your example and live prayerful lives that lead us to grow in holiness. Amen.

© Harcourt Religion

In Unit 1 your child is learning about REVELATION.
CCC *See Catechism of the Catholic Church 51–55, 214 for further reading on chapter content.*

Chapter 2 In the Beginning

Let Us Pray

Leader: Almighty God, we praise you for your glory.
"O Lᴏʀᴅ, our Lord,
how awesome is your name through all
the earth!"

Psalm 8:2

All: Almighty God, we praise you for your glory. Amen.

© Harcourt Religion

Activity — Let's Begin

God's Grandeur

The world is charged with the grandeur of God.
It will flame out, like shining from shook foil;
It gathers to a greatness, like the ooze of
oil. . . .

And for all this, nature is never spent;
There lives the dearest freshness deep
down things;
And though the last lights off the black West
went
Oh, morning, at the brown brink eastward,
springs—
Because the Holy Ghost over the bent
World broods with warm breast and with ah!
bright wings.

Excerpt from the poem by Gerard Manley Hopkins

• What in all of creation most reflects God's
grandeur for you?

Creation Stories

◎ Focus What are the differences between the two creation stories?

There are two stories in the Bible about the beginning of the world and how life came to be. Both of them clearly tell you who created humans, and both help you answer some of life's most important questions.

✝ SCRIPTURE   The Book of Genesis

First Story of Creation

After God created the heavens and earth, the earth was formless and in chaos. Darkness covered the waters, and a wind swept over them. Then God spoke and light appeared, challenging the darkness. God separated the two and called them day and night.

Next, God separated the waters. Now there would be order and boundaries, and a world could take shape. Then God separated land from water and one kind of plant from another.

God created the sun, the moon, and the stars. God created living creatures, releasing birds into the sky and fish into the seas. Then God brought animals into being on the land. God created everything full of goodness.

Yet in addition to all that he had created to fill the earth, God created one more creature that would be like God and would share in God's spirit. God created humans, male and female, and placed all of creation in their care.

Based on *Genesis 1:1–30*

❓ Why did God create human life?

© Harcourt Religion

God Creates Man and Woman

The account in the second chapter of Genesis tells you more about God's creation of human life. In this version, God creates the man before he creates the other creatures. Then God creates the woman.

© Harcourt Religion

✝ SCRIPTURE   The Book of Genesis

Second Story of Creation

First God created the heavens and the earth. At that time the earth was like a parched desert, so God made a stream come out of the ground. Then God took some of the clay from the ground and formed a man. God breathed life into the man, and the man awoke.

God planted a wonderful garden called Eden. God asked the man to work in the garden and to take care of it. Soon God saw that it was not good for the man to be alone. So God created more creatures, bringing them to the man to be named. Each creature was good, but none was the right companion for the man. So God caused the man to sleep and removed one of the man's ribs. From this rib God formed a woman as the man's true partner.

Based on *Genesis 2:4–25*

❓ **What qualities of God are revealed by this passage?**

Activity — Share Your Faith

Reflect: Think about the two creation stories.

Share: With a partner, discuss the similarities of and the differences between the two stories.

Act: On a separate sheet of paper, write the similarities and differences that you and your partner found.

51

Lessons of Creation

◎ **Focus** What are the lessons of the two creation stories?

The two creation stories you have just read are found in Genesis, the first book of the **Old Testament**. This is the part of the Bible that tells the stories of God's people before the time of Jesus. In the two creation stories, God is presented as the powerful Creator who recognizes the goodness of all that he has made.

Both stories of creation are important because they help you understand God's love for humans. The first creation story tells you that God alone created the universe. You also learn that God made humans in his own image. In God's eyes, each person has value and dignity.

In the second creation story, God shows his deep care for the man's loneliness by creating a woman to be the man's true partner. This story shows that men and women were created to work together and share in God's life. Humans are social beings; they need one another. That is why people gather in families and communities. This is all part of God's plan.

Original Holiness

Adam and Eve, as the first man and woman are called, were created by God in a state of original holiness, or grace. They shared in God's life. They lived in harmony with each other, with God, and with all of creation. Adam and Eve were pure of heart and generous, and they delighted in their work of caring for the garden.

❓ **What are some ways that men and women work well together to fulfill God's plan?**

© Harcourt Religion

God and Humans

There are other lessons in the two creation stories. God placed the man and the woman in charge of the earth, but that did not mean that they could do whatever they wanted. God made them stewards, or caretakers, of creation. They shared in God's providence, his loving care for everything that he had made.

You, too, are a responsible steward when you protect the environment and treat other living creatures with kindness. Taking care of yourself—your body, your mind, and your spirit—is another part of caring for creation.

The two stories of creation also teach that God *alone* is the Creator and that humans are his creatures. This means that your most important attitude toward God is a response of praise and adoration. After all, God gave you life, embraces you lovingly every day, and gives you everything you need to live with him for eternity .

❓ **What are some ways to protect the environment?**

❓ **How can you take care of yourself in body, mind, and spirit?**

Words of Faith

The **Old Testament** is the first part of the Bible. It is the story of the Hebrew people before Jesus was born. **Eternity** is time without end and new life beyond death.

Activity — Connect Your Faith

✏️ **Design a Game**   Imagine a video game in which all the choices are good ones and in which there are lots of surprises, but no one gets hurt. What could make a game interesting if no one needed to win? On a separate sheet of paper, design such a game.

© Harcourt Reli

Prayer of Praise

 Let Us Pray

Gather and begin with the Sign of the Cross.

Leader: O Lord, our Lord,
how awesome is your name through all the earth!
You have set your majesty above the heavens!

All: **How awesome is your name through all the earth!**

Leader: When I see your heavens, the work of your fingers,
the moon and stars that you set in place—

All: **How awesome is your name through all the earth!**

Leader: What are humans that you are mindful of them,
mere mortals that you care for them?

All: **How awesome is your name through all the earth!**

Leader: Yet you have made them little less
than a god,
crowned them with glory
and honor.

All: **How awesome is your name
through all the earth!**

Psalm 8:2, 4–6

All: **Amen.**

Leader: Let us pray.
Bow your heads as the leader prays.

All: **Amen.**

Sing together.

Praise and thanksgiving let ev'ryone bring
Unto our God for ev'ry good thing.
All together joyfully sing.

"Praise and Thanksgiving", tr. Traditional
Edith Lovell Thomas

© Harcourt Religion

A **Work with Words** Complete each statement.

1. God created every human soul to live with him for

    _____.

2. The two stories of creation in the Bible are found in the Book of

    _____.

3. God created each person with value and _____.

4. Humans are _____; that is, they are made to relate to one another.

5. Because God is the Creator and you are the created, your most important attitude toward God should be _____.

B **Make Connections** Explain some lessons of the two creation stories.

_____

_____

_____

_____

_____

Activity — Live Your Faith

Create a Collage Look through newspapers and magazines. Find photographs that show aspects of God's creation that are described in the Book of Genesis. Assemble the photographs into a mural or collage. Place the completed picture where it can remind you every day of God's creative love.

© Harcourt Religion

Family Faith

◎ Catholics Believe

■ The stories of creation from the Book of Genesis reveal that God alone created the universe.

■ God created man and woman in his own image to live in harmony with him for all eternity.

✚ SCRIPTURE

Read *Joshua 24:16–28* to learn about others who have renewed their commitment to God.

GO ONLINE www.harcourtreligion.com
For weekly Scripture readings and seasonal resources

Activity

Live Your Faith

Thank Your Family Members   Your ability to honor the dignity of others begins in your family. Each family member is a child of God. God has given each of you special gifts and talents. Place the names of all of your family members in a basket. Then have everyone draw one name and keep it a secret. During the week, each family member should write a note of praise and thanksgiving to the selected person for the gift that he or she brings to your family.

People of Faith

Guido di Pietro was an artist in Florence, Italy, when he entered the Dominican monastery. As a young brother (Fra), he continued to celebrate God's creation in his paintings. He used color in new ways to capture the natural beauty of the world. He was ordained a priest in 1418. Throughout his life he continued to bring people closer to God through his art. He is known as **Fra Angelico** because of his "angelic" moral virtues. In 1984 Pope John Paul II declared Blessed Fra Angelico the patron of artists. His feast day is February 18.

▲ **Blessed Fra Angelico c. 1400–1455**

🌸 Family Prayer

Dear God, help us follow Blessed Fra Angelico by seeing beauty in creation and having faith in God's goodness. We praise you for your greatness. Amen.

© Harcourt Religion

In Unit 1 your child is learning about REVELATION.

CCC *See Catechism of the Catholic Church 279–289, 355–361 for further reading on chapter content.*

Chapter 3 God's Faithfulness

Let Us Pray

Leader: Lord, help us know your love.

"As the heavens tower over the earth,
so God's love towers over the faithful."

Psalm 103:11

All: Lord, help us know your love. Amen.

Activity Let's Begin

Sticky Fingers Justin and Greg have been friends as long as they can remember. They go to the same school and are on the same baseball team.

One day Justin and Greg were building a model airplane. It was difficult to cut the fragile wood into the right shapes. Greg had trouble holding the pieces together while the glue dried. Soon his fingers were covered with glue. Bits of paper and wood shavings stuck to his hands.

Justin thought it was funny. "Look at you!" he exclaimed. "Old sticky fingers! You may as well give up!"

"Why don't you help instead of making fun of me?" yelled Greg, jumping out of his chair. The model slipped out of his hands and crashed to the floor.

• What mistakes are Justin and Greg making in their friendship?

© Harcourt Religion

57

God's Covenant

Focus How does God respond to human disobedience?

When people are friends, they don't say or do the first thing that comes to mind. Each one tries to look at things from the other person's point of view. Here is the story of the first time people acted selfishly. It is from the Book of Genesis.

✝ SCRIPTURE
The Book of Genesis

The First Sin

Life in the Garden of Eden was perfect. No one wanted to change a thing until the day the serpent spoke to Eve. The serpent was clever and wanted to make trouble. It asked the woman about the tree of the knowledge of good and evil. She explained that just touching it meant death. The serpent disagreed. "If you eat from the tree," he told her, "you will be like God." Despite God's warning, the woman ate the fruit and also gave some to Adam to eat.

The man and the woman had chosen not to obey God. Their relationship with God was broken. Their disobedience also broke the relationship between God and all other humans who were to come into existence. Because of their actions, there would be hard labor, pain, and death in the world. However, God did not stop loving humans.

❓ **Why did Adam and Eve eat the fruit of the tree?**

❓ **What "forbidden fruit" do people still eat today?**

© Harcourt Religion

Humans Struggle to Love

The man and woman remained outside the garden. They had two sons, Cain and Abel. Cain was a farmer, and his brother Abel a shepherd. Both made offerings to God, but only Abel's offering pleased God. Abel gave his best sheep to God, but Cain gave only poor products from his field. When God told Cain not to be resentful toward his brother, Cain did not listen. In his anger and jealousy, he killed Abel.

The Great Flood

As more people were born, sin continued. God was grieved with humans because of so much evil. He decided to destroy all creatures in a great flood. Noah, his family, and a certain number of creatures were brought to safety in an ark. After the flood God made a covenant, a sacred agreement joining God and humans together. His covenant was with Noah and all of creation. As a sign of the covenant, God set a rainbow in the sky. It was a sign of his promise that he would never again destroy the earth with a flood. From that time on, God has remained faithful to his covenant. God's **faithfulness** is forever.

Based on *Genesis* 3:1–24, 4:1–15, 7:1–4, 9:8–11

❓ **How does God show his faithfulness and love?**

Words of Faith

Faithfulness is the loyalty and steadfastness that God shows to all humans, even when they sin. God's offer of friendship is never withdrawn.

Activity — Share Your Faith

Reflect: Which of God's actions or characteristics show you his faithfulness to you?

Share: With a partner, discuss these actions or characteristics.

Act: Write the word *faithfulness* vertically on a separate sheet of paper. Use each letter to begin a word or phrase that states an action or characteristic of God that shows his friendship with you.

© Harcourt Religion

Sin and God's Faithfulness

Focus Who is the "new Adam"?

The Book of Genesis tells yet another story of how humans sinned and became separated from one another.

✝ SCRIPTURE The Book of Genesis

The Tower of Babel

In the beginning, everyone spoke the same language. Noah's descendants settled in a beautiful valley. There they decided to build a city and a tower that would reach to the sky. They did this because they were filled with pride and wanted to display their power.

God saw what the people were doing and made their languages different so that no one could understand what anyone else was saying. The place became known as Babel, because it was there that people spoke without being understood. Then God scattered the people all over the earth, and they were unable to communicate with one another because of their different languages.

Based on *Genesis 11:1–9*

Free Will

When the first humans disobeyed God, they committed **original sin**. Because of the first humans' free choice to do wrong, all humans are born with original sin. The tendency to sin, as well as suffering and death, are part of the human experience.

The **temptation** to sin is part of being human. With God's help, you can overcome temptation.

❓ **What is one temptation that young people your age face today?**

© Harcourt Religion

The New Covenant

By their disobedience, the first man and woman brought sin and death into the world. Time after time, God's people broke their covenant with him. But an ever-faithful God made a new covenant with humans.

God the Father fully revealed himself and his faithfulness by sending his own Son. Jesus is the Father's most complete and perfect revelation of God's love for his people. The covenant that God made with Noah and with his chosen people, the Israelites, pointed toward Jesus and is fulfilled in him.

The New Adam

Jesus is called the "new Adam." Jesus makes amends for the disobedience of Adam. Jesus conquered sin and brought everlasting life. When you were baptized, Jesus, through his passion, death, and Resurrection, freed you from original sin and brought you into new life, the very life of God.

❓ **What can you learn about God the Father through the life, death, and Resurrection of his Son?**

© Harcourt Religion

Words of Faith

Original sin refers to the sin of the first humans and its affects on all humans. Sin and death are part of the human condition because of the first humans' choice.

Temptation is an attraction to sin, those actions and omissions that go against right reason and against God's law.

Jesus 2000, Sara Morton

Activity — Connect Your Faith

Plan a Mural Plan a design for a mural that shows one of the main events in the Book of Genesis. Write why that event is important for you today.

Genesis

_____

_____

_____

_____

Prayer for Mercy

Let Us Pray

Gather and begin with the Sign of the Cross.

Leader: Blessed be the Lord

All: **Now and forever.**

Group 1:   Merciful and gracious is the LORD,
slow to anger, abounding in kindness.

Group 2:   As the heavens tower over the earth,
so God's love towers over the faithful.

Group 1:   As far as the east is from the west,
so far have our sins been removed from us.

Group 2:   As a father has compassion on his children,
so the LORD has compassion on the faithful.

Psalm 103:8, 11–13

Leader: Let us pray for God's mercy.

Sing together.

Hold us in your mercy.
Hold us in your mercy.

"Hold Us in Your Mercy: Penitential Litany"
Rory Cooney, © 1993, GIA Publications, Inc.

© Harcourt Religion

Review and Apply

(A) Work with Words   Circle the letter of each correct answer.

1. Sin has been present in the world since the first humans chose to _____.

    a. resist temptation   **b.** disobey God   **c.** name the animals

2. Cain killed his brother, Abel, because _____.

    a. his parents favored Abel   **b.** Cain felt anger and jealousy   **c.** Abel had more sheep

3. The sacred agreement that God made with Noah is called a _____.

    a. rainbow   **b.** trust   **c.** covenant

4. God revealed himself fully by _____.

    a. sending his Son, Jesus   **b.** saving Noah from the flood   **c.** giving the Ten Commandments

5. Jesus conquers sin and brings you everlasting life as the new _____.

    a. Adam   **b.** Noah   **c.** Abel

(B) Check Understanding   Define original sin, and name its effects.

_____

_____

Activity — Live Your Faith

Create an Announcement   Some people forget about God's faithfulness, and some have never heard of it. Create a public service radio announcement or a commercial that will spread this good news. Write the script. Make sure that your announcement or commercial can be read in thirty seconds or less. Perform your announcement or commercial for your class.

_____

_____

_____

_____

© Harcourt Religion

Family Faith

Catholics Believe

- God fully revealed his faithfulness to humans by sending his only Son, Jesus, to conquer sin and bring everlasting life.

- Humans have the ability to live in friendship with God.

SCRIPTURE

Read *Deuteronomy 8:6–20* to learn how you can praise God's goodness and resist temptation.

 www.harcourtreligion.com
For weekly Scripture readings and seasonal resources

Live Your Faith

Make a Choice   When things are not going well, you may be tempted to do the wrong thing. Consider the following family situations and the choices those situations present. If a child is late for school and misses the bus, what might you be tempted to do? What would be a better choice? If a family member breaks a school rule, what might you be tempted to do? What would be a better choice?

People of Faith

▲ **Blessed Peter To Rot 1912–1945**

Peter To Rot was born in a village on the island of Papua, New Guinea. His parents were among the region's first generation of Catholics. In 1930 Peter enrolled at Saint Paul's Mission School for the training of catechists. Soon he became a recognized leader and was assigned to the mission in his own village. When the Japanese invaded the island in 1942, they forbade Christian worship and all religious gatherings. In 1945 Peter was arrested for practicing his faith. He was held in a concentration camp and was eventually killed. Blessed Peter's feast day is July 17.

Family Prayer

Dear God, help us follow Blessed Peter's example by walking with you and living as your faithful servants. Amen.

© Harcourt Religion

In Unit 1 your child is learning about REVELATION.

64   **CCC** *See Catechism of the Catholic Church 396–411, 1468, 1730 for further reading on chapter content.*

A **Work with Words** Solve the puzzle using the clues provided.

Across

4. God's act of bringing all things into being

6. a sacred agreement joining God and humans

9. God's forgiveness and friendship

10. time without end

Down

1. the state of holiness in which God created the first humans

2. first part of the Bible

3. attraction to sin

5. first disobedience against God

7. Scripture and Tradition

8. God's steadfastness

© Harcourt Religion

Unit 2
Trinity

In this unit you will...

learn that God invites all humans on a journey of faith. The Old Testament reveals the way God's people experienced his saving actions on their faith journey. God the Father continued his saving work by sending his Son, Jesus. Jesus teaches us to love as he loves. He establishes a new covenant at the Last Supper, and by his life, death, Resurrection, and Ascension he fulfills the covenant first established with the Israelites.

Chapter 4

Chapter 5

Chapter 6

What do you think you will learn in this unit about your journey of faith?

© Harcourt Religion

Chapter 4 Invitation to Faith

Let Us Pray

Leader: Faithful God, thank you for caring for us.

"My travels and my rest you mark;
with all my ways you are familiar."

Psalm 139:3

All: Faithful God, thank you for caring for us. Amen.

Activity Let's Begin

A Journey   Traveling can be fun. You may be going to see friends or family members whom you have not seen in a long time. You may be taking a train or flying for the first time.

Taking a trip can also be unsettling. You may not know what to pack because you don't know what the weather will be like, or you may be afraid that you will not be able to find the place that you plan to visit.

Your journeys through life can be both exciting and scary. Journeys include both changes and challenges. Because there are often many unknowns, a journey can also include taking some risks.

• Imagine that life is a journey that requires a backpack containing only five things. What five things will you pack? Tell why you will include them.

© Harcourt R

Abram and Sarai's Journey

◎ Focus Who is Abraham?

The risks involved in a journey are not so scary if you know that God is with you. Abram and Sarai learned that God was with them always. They remained faithful to God, and God blessed them.

✝ SCRIPTURE   The Book of Genesis

Abram's Call

Abram and Sarai were getting old and had no children. One day God said to Abram, "Go forth from the land of your kinsfolk and from your father's house to a land that I will show you. I will make you a great nation, and I will bless you."

As God directed, Abram and Sarai took all of their possessions and set out for the land of Canaan. After traveling through the land to a sacred place, Abram had a vision of God, who said, "To your descendants I will give this land." So Abram built an altar there to honor God and continued on the journey with Sarai.

❓ Why would God's words have surprised Abram and Sarai?

© Harcourt Religion

The Journey Continues

God appeared again to Abram and told him that his descendants would be as numerous as the stars in the sky and that they would have a land of their own. Although he had no children, Abram put his faith in God. God changed Abram's name to Abraham and Sarai's name to Sarah as a sign of the covenant.

One day three men visited Abraham and Sarah. The couple quickly prepared a meal for their guests. The men told Abraham that Sarah would have a son, as God had promised. Sarah was listening and laughed to herself because she was too old to have children. But within a year Sarah did give birth to a son and named him Isaac, which means "one who laughs."

Based on *Genesis* 12:1–9; 15:1–6, 18; 17:4–5, 15–16; 18:1–14; 21:1–6

? **How did God keep his promise to Abraham and Sarah?**

Activity — Share Your Faith

Reflect: Think about important qualities that believers share, and unscramble the letters below to discover three of these qualities.

Share: With a partner, share examples of how Abraham and Sarah showed these qualities.

Act: Write one example of each quality from today's world, and present your examples to the class.

1. fitah

_____

2. opeh

_____

3. velo

_____

© Harcourt Religion

God's Plan of Salvation

◎ Focus What does it mean to have faith?

The faith journey that began with Abraham continued with his son Isaac and Isaac's son Jacob. It is from Jacob that the nation of Israel would take its name.

✝ SCRIPTURE

The Book of Genesis

The Story of Joseph

In the Book of Genesis, Jacob was renamed *Israel* after wrestling with an angel. The name means "one who struggles with God."

Jacob became the father of twelve sons, but Joseph was his favorite. Joseph's brothers were jealous of him and plotted to get rid of him. They sold him to a caravan of travelers, and Joseph became a slave. Because he could interpret dreams, Joseph saved Egypt from starvation during a great famine. Joseph's brothers arrived in Egypt to buy food and were united with Joseph, who invited them to settle there.

Based on *Genesis 37–45*

❓ If Joseph's story were made into a movie, what might the title be?

God Invites

As seen through the faith stories of Abraham, Sarah, and their descendants, God keeps his promise of salvation.

You encounter God today through the Bible, the sacraments, and the Church. God's Son, Jesus, is the way of salvation for you. The Holy Spirit, whom Jesus sent, will help you on your faith journey. Wherever you go, God the Father is with you.

God invites you to respond to him in the same way that Abraham and Sarah did—with **faith**. This means that you freely choose to believe in God and all that God has revealed. When you respond to God with faith, you offer your heart and mind to him. You begin your own journey of faith, as Abraham and Sarah did. You have faith that God will guide you and keep his promises to you.

Faith and Prayer

God still speaks to people today, and people can communicate with God. This is done through **prayer**. Prayer begins and ends with listening to God. You can strengthen your faith with prayer, using one of these forms: blessing and adoration, petition for your own needs, intercession (praying for the needs of others), thanksgiving, or praise. You can take time to pray at any time throughout the day.

❓ **When and where are you most comfortable praying?**

❓ **What helps you listen for God's voice?**

Words of Faith

Faith is believing in God and all that God has revealed. Faith is both a gift from God and a free choice.

Prayer is raising your mind and heart to God. In prayer, you both listen and talk to God.

Activity — Connect Your Faith

Choose Gestures   Write the names of the five prayer forms on this page. Choose a prayerful gesture for each form, and share it with your class.

_____

_____

_____

_____

© Harcourt Religion

Celebration of the Word

Let Us Pray

Gather and begin with the Sign of the Cross.

Sing together.

My shepherd is the Lord,
nothing indeed shall I want.

"Psalm 23: My Shepherd Is the Lord"
© 1963, The Grail, GIA Publications, Inc., agent

Leader: The story of the Good Shepherd celebrates the care that Jesus gives to those who say "yes" to a journey of faith with him. We pray that our faith will continue to grow as he leads us.

Reader 1: A reading from the holy Gospel according to John.

Read John 10:14–18.

The Gospel of the Lord.

All: **Praise to you, Lord Jesus Christ.**

Reader 2: My sheep hear my voice; I know them, and they follow me. I give them eternal life, and they shall never perish. No one can take them out of my hand.

Reader 3: My Father, who has given them to me, is greater than all, and no one can take them out of the Father's hand.

John 10:27–29

Leader: Let us pray.

Bow your heads as the leader prays.

All: **Amen.**

Jesus as the Good Shepherd,
Exeter Cathedral, England

© Harcourt Religion

CHAPTER 4

Review and Apply

A **Work with Words**   Complete the following statements.

1. God promised that he would make a great _____ from Abram and his descendants.

2. Sarah gave birth to a son whose name was

   _____ .

3. Jacob received the name _____ , which means "one who struggles with God."

4. The journey that God calls you to make is a journey of

   _____ .

5. _____ is talking to and listening to God.

B **Make Connections**   Write your response to **one** of these questions.

- In what ways did God bless Abraham and Sarah for their faith in him?

- How do you show your own faith in God?

_____

_____

Activity   Live Your Faith

Track Your Journey   Make a time line of your faith journey thus far. Include several significant events, and tell how God was present with you in each one.

© Harcourt Religion

Family Faith

Catholics Believe

- God calls you on a journey of faith toward salvation.

- The path toward salvation is paved with prayer, which allows the Holy Spirit to lead you away from sin.

✝ SCRIPTURE

Read *Romans 1:8–15* to learn about others who praised God for his assistance on their faith journey.

GO ONLINE www.harcourtreligion.com
For weekly Scripture readings and seasonal resources

Activity

Live Your Faith

Plan Your Trip Each person has his or her own journey of faith toward salvation, but your family is also on a journey together. Create a map of your family journey for the next year. Plan some of the stops your family will make along the way on the journey of faith. Plot important events, such as birthdays and holidays, that you foresee along the way.

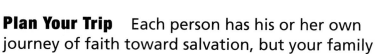

OUR FAITH JOURNEY

People of Faith

▲ Saint Monica
c. 331–387

Monica, a woman of great faith, lived in North Africa. Through Monica's influence, both her husband and mother-in-law were baptized. Monica had a son named Augustine. In his youth, Augustine led a disgraceful life. For many years Monica prayed constantly for his conversion, and her prayers were answered. With God's help, Augustine turned his life around and became a great bishop, writer, and teacher. Today the Church honors him and his mother as saints. Saint Monica's feast day is August 27.

🙌 Family Prayer

Saint Monica, pray for us that we may follow your example of faithful prayer. Remind us to pray for our family members. Amen.

© Harcourt Religion

In Unit 2 your child is learning about the TRINITY.

CCC *See Catechism of the Catholic Church 176–184, 2558–2565 for further reading on chapter content.*

Chapter 5 God's Saving Action

Let Us Pray

Leader: Eternal God, make us open to your presence.
"Blessed be the Lord day by day,
God, our salvation, who carries us."

Psalm 68:20

All: Eternal God, make us open to your presence. Amen.

Activity — Let's Begin

A Hero A hero in a comic book may have big muscles or supernatural powers. A sports hero is admired for his or her physical abilities. A hero in an adventure story is courageous in the face of danger. People look up to heroes and want to be like them.

Heroes are also those who go to work every day and do their jobs. The work they do makes people such as nurses, ambulance drivers, firefighters, and police officers true heroes. Occasionally their names appear in the news. But every day they are heroes.

• Who are your heroes? What qualities do you find heroic?

© Harcourt Religion

God Calls People

◎ Focus How does God save his people?

God calls ordinary people to accomplish extraordinary things. From biblical times to the present, God calls people where they are to do his work.

A REAL-LIFE STORY

September 11, 2001

September 11, 2001, began like any other day. But before it was over, Victoria and Richie had become heroes. Victoria was in the World Trade Center in New York City when she heard shouts and loud noises. It was 8:52 A.M. Terrorists had crashed an airplane into one of the twin towers.

Victoria was the director of a New York train system. She realized that if the tower collapsed, everyone in the train station under the towers would be in great danger. Victoria quickly phoned Richie, the train master, and told him not to let any passengers out at the World Trade Center.

Richie acted right away. He told the train conductors to keep all of the passengers on the trains and to pick up everyone else at the station. By 10:29 A.M. both towers had collapsed. Thanks to Victoria and Richie, thousands of people were saved.

❓ What qualities did Victoria and Richie have that allowed them to respond the way they did?

© Harcourt Religion

God Saves

The Old Testament contains many stories of people whom God called to do extraordinary things. Moses was one of these people. Through him, you can see God's saving power at work.

Moses

After the time of Joseph, the pharaoh of Egypt made the Hebrews his slaves. Despite their slavery, the Hebrews, also called Israelites, grew stronger and more numerous. Finally, the pharaoh ordered every Hebrew boy to be killed.

To save her child, Moses' mother placed him in a basket and floated the basket on the Nile River. The pharaoh's daughter found Moses and raised him in the royal palace.

When Moses was a man, God sent him to the pharaoh to demand freedom for the Hebrews. Moses did as God asked, but the pharaoh refused to listen. God then sent nine plagues to the Egyptians. When the pharaoh still refused, God sent a tenth plague, the angel of death, to kill all of the firstborn Egyptian sons.

Based on *Exodus 1:6—2:10, 7:1—11:10, 12:29*

❓ **What qualities did Moses have that helped him answer God's call?**

Activity — Share Your Faith

Reflect: Reflect on what you already know about how God called Moses.

Share: In a small group, read and discuss *Exodus 3:1–22.*

Act: In the space below, draw a symbol that expresses the message of the reading.

Remembrance Meals

◎ Focus What is the meaning of the Passover meal and the Last Supper?

Faith Fact

In the Old Testament, the name LORD (in capital letters) is the Hebrew word *Yahweh*. *Yahweh* is the name of the God of Israel. In the Hebrew Scriptures, *Yahweh* is written with the four consonants YHWH.

In the Bible, you read about two special meals. In the Old Testament, God commands the Jewish people to remember the Exodus by celebrating the Passover meal. In the New Testament, Jesus tells his followers to remember him in the breaking of bread.

The Passover Meal

Before God sent the final plague, he gave Moses special instructions for the people of Israel. Each family was to kill and eat a lamb and cover the door frame of the home with the lamb's blood. The angel of death would pass over the houses marked with blood, sparing the firstborn sons of the Israelites. On that last night in Egypt, the people had to eat quickly, making bread without yeast to save time.

This great and terrible night is known as the **Passover** of the Lord because it was the night that death passed over the houses of the Israelites. It would be remembered as a new beginning for the people—the night that, through Moses, God delivered them from slavery to freedom. This was the beginning of the **Exodus**.

Since that time, the descendants of the Israelites, later called *Jews*, have eaten a special meal called the *Passover Seder* to remember, make present, and celebrate God's saving power. The people eat bitter herbs to remind them of their ancestors' bitter suffering as slaves in Egypt. They also eat unleavened bread called *matzoh*. Like the bread Moses and his people ate on the first Passover night, matzoh contains no yeast and does not need to rise before it is baked.

The Jewish Passover Seder Meal

❓ How does the Passover meal help people remember the Exodus?

❓ Why is Passover still celebrated by Jews today?

Jesus Saves

God made a covenant with both Moses and the Israelites, an agreement that he would be their God and that they would be his people. When God the Father sent his Son, he made a new covenant with all people forever. This covenant calls for the same kind of faithfulness that the earlier covenant promised. By the grace of the Holy Spirit, you participate in the new covenant every time you take part in the Church's sacraments or make good choices. Because Jesus did his Father's will even in death, God's saving work is completely fulfilled in him.

Like the other Jews of his time, Jesus celebrated God's saving power at a Passover meal. As Jesus blessed bread and wine at the Last Supper, he told the Apostles that the bread and wine were a sign of the new covenant between God and God's people. The bread and wine became Christ's own Body and Blood.

The actions of Jesus at the Passover meal mark the new covenant brought about by Jesus' death and Resurrection, offering salvation to all people who are faithful. The new ritual meal, first shared at the Last Supper, is the Eucharist, which is still celebrated today.

Words of Faith

Passover is the Jewish holy day that celebrates God's leading the Israelites out of slavery in Egypt.

The **Exodus** is the Israelites' journey from slavery in Egypt to freedom in the promised land, accomplished and directed by God.

The **Last Supper** was Jesus' celebration of the Passover meal, with the Apostles. During this supper, Jesus turned the bread and wine into his Body and Blood.

Activity — Connect Your Faith

Compare Ritual Meals With a partner, research the Passover and Eucharistic meals. Find out what foods are eaten at each meal and what is remembered and celebrated. Record the information below.

PASSOVER	EUCHARIST

Prayer of Praise

Let Us Pray

Gather and begin with the Sign of the Cross.

Leader: When Moses and the Israelites were saved from the Egyptians, they responded in song. May their song be our song.

Reader 1: I will sing to the LORD, for he is gloriously triumphant;
    horse and chariot he has cast into the sea.
My strength and my courage is the LORD,
    and he has been my savior.

All: **The LORD shall reign forever and ever.**

Reader 2: In your mercy you led the people you redeemed;
    in your strength you guided them to your holy dwelling.
And you brought them in and planted them
      on the mountain of your inheritance—
the place where you made your seat, O LORD,
    the sanctuary, O LORD, which your hands established.

All: **The LORD shall reign forever and ever.**

Exodus 15:1–2, 13, 17–18

Sing together.

Sing a new song to the Lord,
He to whom wonders belong!
Rejoice in his triumph and tell
    of his power,
O sing to the Lord a new song!

"Sing a New Song to the Lord"
Timothy Dudley-Smith, © 1973,
Hope Publishing Co.

Leader: Let us pray.

*Bow your heads
as the leader prays.*

All: **Amen.**

Ⓐ Work with Words Circle the letter of the correct response.

1. Whom did God send to lead his people out of Egypt?
   a. Jesus **b.** Moses **c.** the pharaoh

2. What is the Israelites' journey from slavery to freedom called?
   a. the ten plagues **b.** the pharaoh's wrath **c.** the Exodus

3. What do Passover and Eucharist celebrate?
   a. God's saving action
   b. God's blessed water
   c. food from heaven

4. When was the Last Supper celebrated?
   a. at the king's meal
   b. at the Passover meal
   c. at the Exodus meal

5. What is the new ritual meal that Jesus celebrated?
   a. the Seder **b.** a sacrifice **c.** the Eucharist

Ⓑ Check Understanding Tell what Jesus did at the Last Supper and how it connects with the celebration of Mass today.

_____

_____

Activity — Live Your Faith

Make a Video Moses was an "action hero" whose faith helped free the Israelites. Design a video of Moses' life. Create three scenes from this chapter. Draw them in the storyboard frames. Tell the class why these scenes would have been important to the Israelites.

Family Faith

Catholics Believe

- God rescued the Hebrews from slavery in Egypt and sent his Son to save all people from the power of sin and everlasting death.

- The Passover and the Eucharist celebrate God's saving actions.

✝ SCRIPTURE

Read *Deuteronomy 31:1–8* to learn what Moses said about courage.

www.harcourtreligion.com
For weekly Scripture readings and seasonal resources

Activity

Live Your Faith

Honor a Hero Do some research on present-day models of courage.

- Look for stories, articles, and books about ordinary people who do extraordinary things.
- Discuss the qualities that these people share.
- Write a letter to one of these heroes, and tell that person what you most admire about him or her.

People of Faith

Edith Stein was born in Germany. When she was in her thirties, Edith became a Catholic and entered a convent. She took the religious name Sister Teresa Benedicta of the Cross. During World War II, she moved to the Netherlands. In the Netherlands, the Nazis began persecuting Jews. Because she was of Jewish origin, Teresa was arrested and sent to the death camp at Auschwitz, where she was executed. Pope John Paul II beatified her in 1987 and named her a saint in 1998. Her feast day is August 9.

▲ Saint Teresa Benedicta 1891–1942

Family Prayer

Saint Teresa, pray for us that we may remain faithful, even during difficult times, and that we may work to overcome prejudice. Amen.

In Unit 2 your child is learning about the TRINITY.

CCC *See Catechism of the Catholic Church 1150–1151, 1339–1340 for further reading on chapter content.*

Chapter 6 Called to Faithfulness

Let Us Pray

Leader: We praise you, we bless you, we thank you, O Lord.

"It is good to give thanks to the LORD,
to sing praise to your name, Most High."

Psalm 92:2

All: We praise you, we bless you, we thank you, O Lord. Amen.

Activity — Let's Begin

Alice in Wonderland   "Get to your places!" shouted the Queen. After running about and tumbling into one another, people finally settled down, and the game began. Alice thought the game was very strange; the balls were live hedgehogs, and the mallets were live flamingoes.

Just as Alice was about to hit a hedgehog with her unusual mallet, the flamingo twisted its neck and looked up into her face. By the time Alice stopped laughing, the hedgehog had unrolled itself and was crawling away. Alice soon came to the conclusion that this was a very difficult game indeed.

Without waiting for turns, everyone played at once, quarreling all the while. Soon the Queen was furious, and she went stamping about, shouting, "Off with his head!" or "Off with her head!" about once every minute.

• What would be the best and worst things about living in Wonderland?

God's Faithful Presence

Focus What did God give the Israelites when he gave them the Ten Commandments?

Having consistent rules would have allowed everyone to get along better in Wonderland. The most important rule of loving and lasting relationships is fidelity, or "faithful presence." God promised the Hebrews that he would be their faithful God and would protect them always. He also asked the Hebrews to be faithful and obedient to his covenant and to his laws.

✝ SCRIPTURE   The Book of Exodus

The Ten Commandments

As the Israelites traveled through the desert, food began to run out. The people complained to Moses that it would have been better to remain as slaves in Egypt than to die of hunger in the desert! God responded by providing quail and a special food called *manna*.

When the water ran out, the people complained again. So God commanded Moses to strike a rock, and water poured out. Even after these miracles, the people of Israel still complained.

God wanted the Israelites to be a holy people who would understand his loving relationship with all creation. When the people reached Mount Sinai, the Lord spoke to Moses at the top of the mountain and gave him the law of the covenant. The cornerstone of the law that God gave to Moses is the Ten Commandments.

Based on *Exodus 16:1–15, 17:1–7, 19:1—20:17*

❓ How did God show his faithfulness to the people?

God's Laws

God knew that his laws would nourish the Israelites even more than the manna and the quail. He knew that his laws would strengthen their relationships. The Ten Commandments appear in the Bible in both the Book of Exodus and the Book of Deuteronomy. The Ten Commandments are also called the Decalogue, which means "ten words." The Ten Commandments are listed in your Catholic Source Book.

The Commandments reflect the heart of the covenant. With these words God called the people of Israel to respect the holiness of the Lord and also to see holiness in themselves.

The Commandments were revealed by God, but they also express a common-sense law that is written in the human heart. That law, called the natural moral law, is unchangeable because it rests on an order that is present in all creation. The natural moral law is based on God's eternal law.

God also gave his people other rules, which are contained in the *Torah,* or the first five books of the Bible. *Torah* means "law" or "doctrine." It contains stories that tell how God wants people to live and be faithful to him.

Words of Faith

The **Decalogue** is the Ten Commandments, laws that God gave Moses. The first three commandments have to do with the relationship between God and the people. The other seven commandments help people respect one another.

Activity

Share Your Faith

Reflect: Read *Exodus 20:1–17.*

Share: With a partner, write what each commandment tells you to do.

Act: Choose one commandment that you will focus on following every day this week.

YOU SHALL . . .

Jesus' New Law

Focus How do the Ten Commandments compare with the teaching of Jesus?

Even after Moses received the Ten Commandments from God, the people of Israel sometimes chose to disobey God. But their covenant with God helped the Israelites grow as a people as they wandered in the desert for forty years before crossing into the promised land.

Through the new covenant, all faithful people are promised a place in the kingdom of God. You find your place in God's kingdom when you walk by faith in God through Jesus.

The Teaching of Jesus

Jesus respected the Ten Commandments and used them as a starting point for his own teaching. Then Jesus spoke of another law that included all other commandments. He said, "I give you a new commandment: love one another. As I have loved you, so you also should love one another" (*John 13:34*). This new commandment means that followers of Jesus will live by the Ten Commandments if they love God and others, including their enemies, as Jesus did.

For those who are faithful to Jesus' new law of love, God promises everlasting life and happiness with him in heaven. The Holy Spirit was sent to help you believe in Jesus and live the law of love.

? **What can you do to love others, even your enemies? Give an example.**

Jesus and the Commandments

Compare the words of Jesus with some of God's "ten words." Describe the similarities and differences you see.

DECALOGUE	WORDS OF JESUS
I am the Lord, your God. You shall not have strange gods before me.	You shall love the Lord, your God, with all your heart, with all your soul, and with all your mind *(Matthew 22:37)*.
You shall not take the name of the Lord in vain.	But I say to you, do not swear at all *(Matthew 5:34)*.
Remember to keep holy the Lord's day.	The sabbath was made for man, not man for the sabbath *(Mark 2:27)*.
You shall not bear false witness against your neighbor.	But whoever lives the truth comes to the light, so that his works may be clearly seen as done in God *(John 3:21)*.
You shall not covet your neighbor's goods.	One's life does not consist of possessions *(Luke 12:15)*.

Activity — Connect Your Faith

Design a T-Shirt Develop a motto for a "Commandments T-Shirt." Create a catchy phrase that tells how to obey one of the commandments.

Celebration of the Word

Let Us Pray

Gather and begin with the Sign of the Cross.

Leader: The Ten Commandments and Jesus' new law of love help us be faithful to God, ourselves, and others. Imagine that we are gathered with Jesus and the Apostles at the Last Supper. Listen to and reflect on Jesus' words to us.

Reader: A reading from the holy Gospel according to John.

Read John 15:11–17.

Reader: The Gospel of the Lord.

All: **Praise to you, Lord Jesus Christ.**

Leader: We turn our hearts and minds to God and ask him to bless those who love us and those whom we love.

Pray aloud your intercessions one by one. After each, respond

All: **Lord, hear the prayer of your faithful ones.**

Sing together.

This is my commandment, that you love one another that your joy may be full. This is my commandment, that you love one another that your joy may be full, that your joy may be full, that your joy may be full. This is my commandment, that you love one another that your joy may be full.

"This Is My Commandment," Traditional

Leader: Let us pray.

Bow your heads as the leader prays.

All: **Amen.**

Review and Apply

A **Work with Words**   Complete the following statements.

1. The Ten Commandments are also called the _____.

2. The Israelites called the first five books of the Bible the _____.

3. God asks you for your _____ to his covenant and laws.

4. The common-sense law that is written in your heart is called the _____.

5. The new commandment that Jesus gave his followers is _____.

B **Check Understanding**   Write a brief summary of the chapter that includes the four terms listed here:

fidelity   **natural moral law**
Decalogue   **Jesus' new commandment**

_____

_____

_____

_____

_____

Activity Live Your Faith

Role-Play Responses   Gather in small groups. Describe a real-life situation that someone your age might face because he or she follows or ignores one of the Ten Commandments. Role-play a Christian response to the situation. Share your group's results with the larger group.

Family Faith

⊙ Catholics Believe

- The Ten Commandments help you stay close to God and in right relationship with others.

- The Ten Commandments are the laws of God's covenant with the Israelites, which was revealed in its fullness in Jesus.

✝ SCRIPTURE

Read *Deuteronomy 5:1–21* and compare its wording to the wording in *Exodus 20:1–17*.

GO ONLINE www.harcourtreligion.com
For weekly Scripture readings and seasonal resources

Activity

Live Your Faith

Discuss House Rules God gave you the Ten Commandments to establish rules of conduct and to help you enjoy good relationships with him and with others. What rules of conduct does your family have? Why are these rules important?

Family Rules
1.
2.
3.
4.
5.

People of Faith

▲ Saint Teresa of Ávila 1515–1582

Teresa was born in Spain into a large noble family of Jewish ancestry. After she had been a nun in a Carmelite monastery for twenty years, she felt God calling her to a special task. Teresa then dedicated herself to reforming many Carmelite convents in Spain, making them stronger and more faith-filled. Teresa was one of the first women to write about the spiritual life. Her writings are still read and treasured today. Teresa was declared a saint forty years after her death. In 1970 she was named a doctor (great teacher of faith) of the Church. Her feast day is October 15.

👐 Family Prayer

Saint Teresa, pray for us that we may follow your example of listening for God's call and acting in faith and prayer. Amen.

In Unit 2 your child is learning about the TRINITY.

CCC *See Catechism of the Catholic Church 1949–1953, 1961–1966 for further reading on chapter content.*

UNIT 2 REVIEW

A **Work with Words**   Complete the following statements.

1. The laws that God first gave to Moses are called the _____, or the Ten Commandments.

2. The Jewish holy day that celebrates God's leading the Israelites out of slavery in Egypt is called _____.

3. _____ is both a gift from God and a free choice.

4. During the _____ _____, Jesus turned the bread and wine into his Body and Blood.

5. Directed and accomplished by God, the _____ is the Israelites' journey from slavery in Egypt to freedom in the promised land.

B **Check Understanding**   Circle the letter of the choice that best completes each sentence.

6. The ritual meal first shared at the Last Supper is the _____.

   a. Mass   **b.** Eucharist

   c. Passover   **d.** Great Feast

7. The natural moral law is based on _____.

   a. the human heart   **b.** the Scriptures

   c. God's eternal law **d.** common sense

8. The Sabbath was made for _____.

   a. man   **b.** all creatures

   c. God   **d.** priests

9. The name *Israel* means _____.

   a. "one who laughs" **b.** "one who struggles with God"

   c. "one who leads"   **d.** "one who loves God"

10. On the night of the Passover, the people of Israel ate bread without _____.

    a. water   **b.** butter

    c. yeast   **d.** any other food

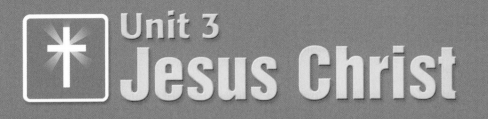

Unit 3
Jesus Christ

In this unit you will...

learn that God chose leaders for his people during Old Testament times who were anointed as priests, prophets and kings. The gospels in the New Testament proclaim that Jesus was also anointed by God to be priest, prophet and king. He is the Messiah whom the prophets spoke of, and God promised to send to his people.

Chapter 7

Chapter 8

Chapter 9

What do you think you will learn in this unit about Jesus, the Savior?

7 Leaders for God's People

Let Us Pray

Leader: God, we thank you for those who lead us to you.

"Your reign is a reign for all ages,
your dominion for all generations."

Psalm 145:13

All: God, we thank you for those who lead us to you. Amen.

Activity — Let's Begin

A Good Leader Hiking up a wooded mountain trail can be quite an adventure. But a good adventure depends on guides who can lead you safely to your destination. Good leaders are also essential for families, schools, businesses, churches, and governments.

Good leaders are guides who give directions, urge caution when necessary, and help manage changes along the way. Through their ideas, personalities, and examples, good leaders earn your trust and make you want to follow them. In this way, leaders serve as role models.

• What are the most important qualities of good leaders?

New Leaders

Focus How did Israel get its first king?

Moses had many of the qualities of a strong leader. But Moses died just before the Israelites entered the promised land. Who would be the new leader?

A STORY

The Bible Research Team

Ms. Gomez asked her class to read through the Books of Joshua, Judges, Samuel, and Kings.

"Who followed Moses as leader?" asked Ms. Gomez.

"I know!" said Jamal. "After Moses died, Joshua led the Israelites across the Jordan River into Canaan. God chose Joshua because he was a good military leader and because he trusted God." Jamal explained that under Joshua, the people fought the tribes of Canaan and defeated them. After Joshua's death, heroes arose to lead the tribes.

The Period of Judges

"That's where I pick up," Shannon said. "The local heroes were called judges. Gideon and Jephthah are two judges who were military leaders. Other judges, such as Samuel and Deborah, were prophets."

Gracie continued. "Israel wasn't governed by human power, but by God alone. But the people of Israel were not always happy about this. They wanted a human king."

❓ **Why do you think the Israelites wanted a human king?**

Israel's First King

Justin added, "The last judge of Israel, the prophet Samuel, thought that the Israelites were very foolish to reject God as their only king. Samuel warned the people that the king they wanted would have power over them. But he knew that God would give his people the freedom to find out for themselves."

"So," said Eldon, "God sent Samuel to **anoint** Saul with oil as the first king of Israel. This anointing showed that Saul was God's choice to be king. Saul was strong, tall, and very handsome. He seemed to be the sort of king that the people of Israel were looking for."

"Was Saul a good king?" Ms. Gomez asked.

"Saul became a great military leader," said Kelly. "But he didn't always obey God's commands, and soon his armies began to be defeated. Saul became angry and lost his popularity with the people."

"Then what happened?" the teacher asked.

"God told Samuel to find someone new to anoint as king," replied Kelly. "I think that's where we ended our research."

Words of Faith

To **anoint** is to use oil to mark someone as chosen for a special purpose. In biblical times, the priests, the kings, and sometimes the prophets were anointed as a sign of God's favor.

Activity — Share Your Faith

Reflect: Why do you follow others?

Share: With two other students, discuss why the Israelites followed their leaders.

Act: Look up one of the following passages. Then write the qualities of the leader you read about.

Judges 4:1–16 (Deborah) _____

_____

Judges 6:1–24 (Gideon) _____

_____

Judges 11:11–28 (Jephthah) _____

_____

A Family of Kings

Focus Why is Jesus called the Son of David?

God sent Samuel to Bethlehem to look for the new king who would replace Saul. Here is the story of how the new king was chosen.

✝ SCRIPTURE The Books of 1 Samuel and 2 Samuel

King David

Jesse's seven oldest sons were impressive, but Samuel rejected them all. God had told him not to judge from appearances.

Jesse's youngest son, David, was tending sheep. He was a humble shepherd, a poet, and a harp player. Jesse thought that David was too young to be chosen as king, but Samuel asked to see David anyway. When the boy arrived, God told Samuel that David was the one who would be king. Samuel anointed David with oil as the boy's brothers watched. From that day on, God's Spirit was with David. David became a leader in Saul's army. Later, after the death of Saul, the men of Judah anointed David as their king.

When David took over from Saul, he united the northern and southern tribes under his rule and made Jerusalem their capital.

David was a great king who tried to understand God's will. He was a model for other leaders of God's people.

Because of David's faithfulness, God renewed the covenant with him. God promised to establish a dynasty, or line of rulers, that would start with David. One day, someone from David's house would be chosen to sit on the royal throne forever.

Based on 1 Samuel 16:1–13; 2 Samuel 2:1–7, 7:8–17

❓ How did David set a good example for God's people?

Jesus, Son of David

A thousand years after David ruled, Jesus was born and fulfilled the promises made to David. Christians believe that Jesus is the King of Kings and that his reign will last forever.

Jesus was like King David in many ways, although David sinned and Jesus was without sin. Jesus' foster father, Joseph, was a descendant of King David. Jesus was born in Bethlehem, where David had lived when God called him through Samuel. Like David, Jesus was a shepherd to God's people and called himself the Good Shepherd.

Both David and Jesus were anointed. In fact, the title *Christ* means "anointed one." God the Father anointed his Son with the Holy Spirit to be prophet, priest, and king. Both David and Jesus were great kings, but only Jesus is king for all eternity.

❓ **What are some ways that Jesus is a shepherd to those who follow him?**

Men of Prayer

Both David and Jesus were men of prayer. David is credited with writing some of the **psalms** you sing today in the Church's liturgy. Jesus prayed often to his Father and taught his followers how to pray. The Lord's Prayer that Jesus taught is one of the first prayers Christians learn today.

Words of Faith

The **psalms** are poems and hymns that were first used in the liturgy of the Israelites. Today the psalms are also prayed and sung in the public prayer of the Church.

An early Christian fresco of Jesus as the Good Shepherd

Activity — **Connect Your Faith**

Prepare a Speech   Prepare and give a short speech in which you tell the class why you would make a good Catholic leader. Give specific examples of your "wisdom."

I would make a good Catholic leader because _____

_____

_____

_____

_____

VOTE FOR ME

Prayer of Praise

Let Us Pray

Gather and begin with the Sign of the Cross.

Sing together.

Alleluia, alleluia, alleluia!

"People of God / Alleluia", David Haas, © 1982, 1991, 1997, GIA Publications, Inc.

Leader: Praised be the Lord.

All: **Now and for ever.**

Leader: Jesus, Son of David, be with us as
we praise you.

Group 1:   My heart is steadfast, God;
my heart is steadfast.
I will sing and chant praise.

Group 2:   Awake, my soul; awake, lyre and harp!
I will wake the dawn.

All: **Alleluia, alleluia, alleluia!**

Group 1:   I will praise you among the peoples, Lᴏʀᴅ;
I will chant your praise among
the nations.

Group 2:   For your love towers to the heavens;
your faithfulness, to the skies.

Psalm 108:2–5

All: **Alleluia, alleluia, alleluia!**

Leader: Let us pray.

Bow your heads as the leader prays.

All: **Amen.**

A **Work with Words** Complete each statement.

1. After the death of Moses, _____ led the people of Israel into the promised land of Canaan.

2. Christians believe that _____ fulfilled the promises made to David.

3. The last judge of Israel was _____. He anointed both Saul and David as kings of Israel.

4. Many sung prayers found in the Bible are called

   _____.

5. The word *Christ* means _____.

B **Check Understanding** Tell what you learned in this chapter about the qualities of a good leader.

_____

_____

_____

Activity Live Your Faith

Design a Poster
God needs wise men and women to lead his people in every age. Design a poster to let others know what qualities a person must have to be a good leader today.

HELP WANTED

Family Faith

Catholics Believe

- In Old Testament times, God chose leaders like Saul and David, who were anointed kings.
- God the Father anointed his Son Jesus with the Holy Spirit to be prophet, priest, and king.

SCRIPTURE

Read *Exodus 18:13–26* to learn one of the ways that Moses became a great leader.

www.harcourtreligion.com
For weekly Scripture readings and seasonal resources

Activity

Live Your Faith

Take a Walk Leaders must be responsible and trustworthy. Go on a "trust walk" as a family. Take turns being the leader. Place a blindfold on one member of the family, and lead that person for part of the walk. Continue until everyone has had a chance to be both leader and follower. Then discuss your experiences. What was hard and what was easy about being in each role?

People of Faith

Born into a wealthy family in Ireland, Catherine McAuley worked all of her life to help those in need. Catherine realized that young servant girls needed to be educated. She helped them make better lives for themselves. Catherine also looked after a wealthy older couple who supported her good works. After the couple died, Catherine inherited their money. She used it to start the Sisters of Mercy, who follow her example of helping those who are poor, especially women.

▲ Venerable Catherine McAuley 1778–1841

Family Prayer

Loving God, help us imitate Venerable Catherine by being leaders in kindness and charity. Help us use our resources to help others. Amen.

In Unit 3 your child is learning about JESUS CHRIST.

CCC *See Catechism of the Catholic Church 59–64, 218–220, 695 for further reading on chapter content.*

Chapter 8 God's Wisdom

Let Us Pray

Leader: Teach us your wisdom, O Lord.

"Still, you insist on sincerity of heart;
in my inmost being teach me wisdom."

Psalm 51:8

All: Teach us your wisdom, O Lord. Amen.

Activity — Let's Begin

A Wise Person "Dad, who's the wisest person in the Wyse family?" asked Roger, as he looked at the portraits on the bookshelf.

"I know!" Roger's sister Emily said. "Aunt Frieda's a doctor. She must be the smartest."

"What about Eduardo?" suggested their brother Gavin. "He runs a business and makes a lot of money. He must be smart, too."

"I think Great-Grandma Annie was the wisest," said Roger's father.

"But she never even finished high school," the kids protested.

"No, but she kept the family together during difficult times. She lived her faith every day."

"Is that what being wise means?" asked Roger.

• Whom do you consider to be a wise person? What qualities does this person have?

God Gives Wisdom

Focus What is wisdom?

God is the source of all wisdom. Wisdom is a gift that God gives us. Here is an Asian folktale about wisdom.

A TALE

A Wise Old Woman

Once there was an old woman who came upon a beautiful red stone in a forest. She had no need for the stone, but she sensed something important about it and put it in her bag. As she was falling asleep that night, she heard someone shout, "You have a very valuable stone. I must have it!"

"What stone might that be?" inquired the woman calmly.

"Last night," said the man, "I dreamed that an old woman would give me a stone that would make me a rich man."

The old woman said, "God must have meant it to be yours."

Surprised, the man took the stone. The next morning the man returned. "I've been thinking," he said. "Only the wisdom that enabled you to give up this stone so easily will make me truly rich. Please give me that wisdom."

The wise woman smiled at him. "You are well on your way to wisdom. You realize that wealth comes not from things but from what you do with them. Keep the stone and use it as God directs you. In time, it will bring you true wisdom."

❓ **What wisdom did the woman show by giving the man the stone she had found?**

Wisdom in the Bible

The old woman knew that riches were not as important as wisdom. **Wisdom** was greatly admired by the people of Israel. They believed that if you did what was right, you would prosper; but if you did what was foolish or evil, you would suffer. A number of the books of the Old Testament contain collections of the wisdom of the people of Israel: the Psalms, Job, Proverbs, Sirach, Ecclesiastes, and Wisdom.

These books in the Bible offer guides for living. The Book of Proverbs is filled with teachings and short sayings that reflect the traditional insights of the people of Israel. You may have heard some of them.

Words of Faith

Wisdom is a gift from God that helps you understand his purpose and plan for your life.

Like the man who seizes a passing dog
　　by the ears
　　　is he who meddles in a quarrel
　　　　not his own.

Proverbs 26:17

The way of the fool seems right in his own eyes,
　　but he who listens to advice is wise.

Proverbs 12:15

Rich and poor have a common bond:
　　the LORD is the maker of them all.

Proverbs 22:2

Gray hair is a crown of glory;
　　it is gained by virtuous living.

Proverbs 16:31

As one face differs from another,
　　so does one human heart from another.

Proverbs 27:19

❓ **What does each of these proverbs mean to you?**

❓ **Which ones have you found to be true in your own life?**

Activity — Share Your Faith

Reflect: Think of someone you know who is wise.

Share: In the Book of Proverbs, find a proverb that suits the person you have chosen, and read the proverb to the class.

Act: Fill out the postcard on the right, and give or send it to the person you chose.

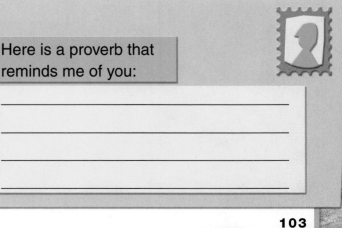

Here is a proverb that reminds me of you:

_____

_____

_____

_____

Wisdom Books

◎ Focus How is God's wisdom shown by Solomon and Job?

The Book of Wisdom, often called the Book of Solomon, teaches in a different way. It is a narrative about the importance of acting wisely.

Solomon, the son of King David, succeeded his father as king. Solomon built a temple in Jerusalem to give the people of Israel a place where they could worship the one true God. However, Solomon is remembered even more for his wisdom.

✝ SCRIPTURE
The Book of 1 Kings

Solomon's Request

Solomon asked for God's help. "I am young," he said. "So that I may serve you well, Lord, give me an understanding heart to judge your people and to know right from wrong."

God approved Solomon's request and replied, "Because you have not asked for wealth and power over your enemies, I will grant your request. I give you the wisest heart that has ever been or will ever be, and I will give you wealth, honor, and long life besides."

Based on 1 Kings 3:4–14

Solomon knew that true wisdom comes from more than human insight. God's laws revealed his purpose and plan. Observing God's laws led to wisdom. Because of his faith, Solomon knew that true human wisdom is a participation in God's own wisdom and goodness.

❓ What gifts should world leaders ask for today?

❓ How would each of these gifts help them?

© Harcourt Religion

A New Way of Seeing

The Books of Wisdom and Proverbs primarily hand down traditional wisdom. Other books, like the Book of Job, challenge popular beliefs.

✝ S C R I P T U R E   **The Book of Job**

The Story of Job

Job was depressed. He was a very good man, yet he was suffering. Some friends told him that his troubles must be his punishment for displeasing God. But Job knew that he was good and demanded to talk to God directly.

God spoke to Job. Revealing all of his creative power and might, he reminded Job of who God is. A terrified Job responded with these words (*Job 42:2–6*):

I know that you can do all things,
   and that no purpose of yours can be hindered.
I have dealt with great things that I do not understand;
   things too wonderful for me, which I cannot know.
I had heard of you by word of mouth,
   but now my eye has seen you.
Therefore I disown what I have said,
   and repent in dust and ashes.

God told Job's friends that they were wrong in what they told Job. He restored Job's health and his prosperity.

Based on the Book of Job

Job, **Jusepe de Ribera**

❓ **What does the writer of the Book of Job want you to understand?**

Activity   Connect Your Faith

✏️ **Compare Ideas**   Gather in small groups. Discuss the meaning of the words *knowledge* and *wisdom.* On a separate sheet of paper, draw a Venn diagram (two overlapping circles). Place in the left area the points that are true only of knowledge, in the right area those true only of wisdom, and in the center area those true of both.

Prayer of Praise

Let Us Pray

Gather and begin with the Sign of the Cross.

Leader:	Lord, open our lips.
All:	**And our mouths will proclaim your praise.**
Reader:	A reading from the Book of Ecclesiastes.
	Read Ecclesiastes 3:1–8.
	The word of the Lord.
All:	**Thanks be to God.**
Leader:	Let us pray.
	Bow your heads as the leader prays.
All:	**Amen.**

Sing together.

We are walking by faith,
   we are walking by faith,
we are walking by faith
   to the kingdom!
In prayer we will
   listen, in your
   wisdom we
   will grow;
we will walk by faith
   till we come to the
   promised land!

"Walking by Faith", David Haas,
© 1997, 2001, GIA Publications, Inc.

Review and Apply

A **Check Understanding**   Circle True if a statement is true, and circle False if a statement is false. Correct any false statements.

1. The wisdom tradition in the Bible is contained primarily in the prophetic books.

   True   False   _____

2. Human wisdom is useless without a reverent trust in God and respect for his law.

   True   False   _____

3. One of the greatest examples of a wise person in the Old Testament was King Saul.

   True   False   _____

4. The Book of Proverbs is an example of wisdom literature.

   True   False   _____

5. God restored Job's health and prosperity.

   True   False   _____

B **Make Connections**   How does a Christian grow in wisdom?

_____

_____

_____

Activity   Live Your Faith

God's Wisdom Lives Today

List Wise Sayings   Make a list of wise sayings that you want to make a part of your life. Write each saying on an individual note card or self-sticking note. Decorate the notes, and post them where they will remind you how to live.

_____

_____

_____

_____

Family Faith

◎ Catholics Believe

■ The wisdom tradition in the Bible teaches that true wisdom comes from trusting God and obeying his law.

■ Jesus is the wisdom of God, sought in every age by those who are wise.

✝ SCRIPTURE

Read *2 Chronicles 1:7–12* to discover why God agreed to grant Solomon's request for wisdom.

GO ONLINE **www.harcourtreligion.com**
For weekly Scripture readings and seasonal resources

Activity
Live Your Faith

Find Wisdom at Home The Book of Proverbs is a collection of wise sayings that show the wisdom of the people. What are the wise sayings of members of your family? Collect some of them in a memory book, and decorate the pages. Add pictures of those who have used these sayings. Keep the book in a special place, and read from it on special occasions.

People of Faith

▲ Saint Ignatius of Loyola 1491–1556

Ignatius was a soldier and a sinner. While recovering from a wound, he experienced conversion. God called Ignatius to win people's minds and hearts for God. Ignatius founded an order called the Society of Jesus. His motto was: "Do everything for the honor and glory of God." The members of the Society of Jesus, who are called Jesuits, became famous for their learning and teaching. They continue their work today in parishes, high schools, and universities. Saint Ignatius's feast day is July 31.

🙌 Family Prayer

Saint Ignatius, pray for us that we may do everything for God's honor and glory. May we always be learning from God's word. Amen.

In Unit 3 your child is learning about JESUS CHRIST.

Chapter 9 The Promised One

Let Us Pray

Leader: Loving God, help us know more of your love.

"Let your love come to me, LORD,
salvation in accord with your promise."

Psalm 119:41

All: Loving God, help us know more of your love. Amen.

Activity Let's Begin

An Important Message Maria had been sick for a week. She had lost her voice and had to use a pencil and paper to communicate.

Finally, her mother decided to give Maria a bell. Now Maria could ring the bell whenever she wanted to call for her mother's help.

Maria's Uncle Carlos helped, too. He taught Maria some sign language. He showed Maria how to use hand gestures to say "I'm hungry," "more," "please," and "thank you." Maria was eager to go back to school to show her friends the sign language she had learned.

• Think of a time when you have helped communicate a message. What message did you deliver? How did you know that your message was understood?

God's Messengers

◎ Focus What message did the prophets bring to the people?

Faith Fact

Babylon was captured in 539 B.C. by the Persian king Cyrus, who allowed the people of Israel to return home.

Even when people haven't lost their voices, they may have trouble communicating because others refuse to listen. Beginning around the time of the kings of Israel, God called certain people to speak the truth to the people and to summon them back to God. These people were called prophets. A **prophet** reminds people to be faithful to the covenant.

One person at the royal court, writing after the death of Solomon, might have written a letter like this one.

A STORY

THE DISTURBER OF ISRAEL

Dear Cousin Abi,

So much has been happening here at the royal court. The kingdom has split in two, with Israel in the north and Judah in the south. But the big news is about prophets.

Since the kingdom has been divided, there have been many false prophets. They speak for money or personal gain. And the court prophets just try to please their kings.

Recently, however, a prophet named Elijah appeared in Israel. He has warned of years of drought to come. King Ahab called Elijah "the disturber of Israel." But Elijah replied that the true disturber of Israel is King Ahab's own household, because his family members worship idols.

What Elijah says is true. The people and rulers are turning away from God. I hope people listen to Elijah soon.

Your loving cousin,

Hanani

❓ What would be hard about being a prophet?

Repentance and Restoration

The people did not listen to Elijah. God continued to send prophets. In the north the prophet Amos criticized those who were wealthy for ignoring those who were poor. Hosea called the people of Israel unfaithful because they had other gods. Micah urged people to turn from their sinful ways back to God. But despite all the warnings, the people did not repent, and the Assyrians conquered Israel, the northern kingdom, in 721 B.C.

In the south the great prophets Isaiah and Jeremiah also tried to reach people with God's message. Isaiah's prophecies predicted punishment for the kingdom. Jeremiah predicted destruction if the people did not repent. The people did not change their ways, however. Jerusalem fell to the Babylonians in 586 B.C. Many of the people of Judah were sent into exile far away.

Byzantine art of prophets, Silvio Fiore

The prophet Ezekiel saw the exile of the people of Israel as God's correction of their wrongdoings. In a prophecy called the Vision of the Dry Bones, Ezekiel shared a picture of the exile and what would come after it. The people understood the prophecy to mean that God would restore them to their land.

Words of Faith

A **prophet** is a messenger from God who speaks the truth and calls the people to justice.

Activity — Share Your Faith

Reflect: Read one of the passages below, and think about what the prophet means.

Isaiah 3:1–8	*Hosea 12:1–4*
Jeremiah 19:10–11	*Amos 8:4–12*
Ezekiel 37:1–14	*Micah 3:9–12, 6:8*

Share: Discuss the prophecy with a partner.

Act: Act out for the class what the prophet is trying to tell the people.

Prophetic Promise

Focus Who is the promised messiah?

The prophets continued to speak to the people even after the Israelites returned to their homeland. Many of the prophetic messages told the people that God would send a **messiah**, God's anointed or chosen one, to save the people. Christians believe that these prophecies of a messiah tell about Jesus.

✝ SCRIPTURE

The Books of Isaiah and Zechariah

The Chosen One

For a child is born to us, a son is given us;
   upon his shoulder dominion rests.
They name him Wonder-Counselor, God-Hero,
   Father-Forever, Prince of Peace.

Isaiah 9:5

Rejoice heartily, O daughter Zion,
   shout for joy, O daughter Jerusalem!
See, your king shall come to you;
   a just savior is he,
Meek, and riding on an ass,
   on a colt, the foal of an ass.

Zechariah 9:9

❓ **What are the similarities and differences between these two prophecies?**

Our Lady of Czestochowa, Byzantine icon

Jesus the Christ

When Jesus began teaching and healing, many in Israel believed that he was the promised one. Jesus is called *Christ,* a word meaning "anointed one" or "messiah." In time his followers also came to understand that Jesus was the Son of God. Through Jesus and in the Holy Spirit, all people share in God's promise of eternal life.

Prophets for Today

God still needs messengers to call people to be faithful and turn away from evil. Here are stories about two of God's messengers.

BIOGRAPHIES

RAY HERMAN

Ray Herman was a priest who worked as a missionary in Bolivia, South America. Father Ray worked with peasant farmers, who were the poorest and most oppressed people in the country. He trained catechists and taught the people farming techniques. He also set up a medical clinic and hospital. He made some people angry with his messages of hope to people who were poor. On October 20, 1975, after blessing the new hospital, Father Herman returned to his parish house. He was attacked and murdered in his sleep.

DOROTHY DAY

When Dorothy Day was thirty, she became a Catholic. Together with her spiritual adviser, Peter Maurin, she founded the Catholic Worker movement. She started soup kitchens for those who were homeless. Until her death in 1980, she chose to live in poverty and was a witness to Jesus' message of love for all who are poor and homeless.

❓ **What qualities did Father Ray and Dorothy Day have in common?**

Words of Faith

The **messiah** was the promised one who would lead his people. The word *messiah* means "God's anointed," or "God's chosen one."

Activity Connect Your Faith

Find the Message Think of someone from the past or present who could be called a prophet. Write the person's name and make up three titles that describe the person's message. Then choose a title that describes your own message.

1. _____

2. _____

3. _____

Me: _____

_____

Prayer of Praise

 Let Us Pray

Gather and begin with the Sign of the Cross.

Sing together.

Prepare the way of the Lord
Prepare the way of the Lord,
and all people will see the salvation
of our God.

"Prepare the Way of the Lord" © 1984, Les Presses de Taizé,
GIA Publications, Inc., agent

Leader: Gracious God, you sent John the Baptist to prepare the way for your Son, Jesus. Today we raise our voices with Zechariah.

Group 1: Blessed be the Lord, the God of Israel, for he has saved his people.

Group 2: He brought salvation through David, as the prophets promised.

Group 1: He showed mercy to our fathers and remembered his covenant with Abraham.

Group 2: This child, John, will be called the prophet of the Most High, for he will prepare the way for the Lord, who will bring his people salvation.

Group 1: The promised one will forgive our sins because of the mercy of God and will shine on all who sit in darkness to guide us to the path of peace.

Based on *Luke 1:68–79*

All: **Blessed be the Lord.**

Review and Apply

A **Work with Words**   Match each description in Column 1 with the correct term in Column 2.

Column 1

_____ 1. the "disturber of Israel"

_____ 2. communicated God's message to others

_____ 3. Israelites taken to Babylon

_____ 4. the anointed of God

_____ 5. turn from sin to God

Column 2

a. exile

b. repent

c. messiah

d. Elijah

e. prophets

B **Check Understanding**   How would you tell the difference between a good prophet and a false prophet?

_____

_____

_____

_____

Activity — Live Your Faith

Write a Poem   Read the Canticle of Mary in *Luke 1:46–55.* Write your own poem, modeling it on Mary's canticle. In your poem, describe what God the Father, the Son, and the Holy Spirit are accomplishing in your life and in the world around you.

_____

_____

_____

_____

_____

_____

Family Faith

◎ Catholics Believe

- **Prophets of the Old Testament spoke for God, telling people to repent and obey God's laws.**
- **Christians believe that Jesus is the Messiah described by the Old Testament prophets.**

✝ SCRIPTURE

Read *1 Timothy 4:6–16* to find Paul's advice for living Christian values.

www.harcourtreligion.com
For weekly Scripture readings and seasonal resources

Activity
Live Your Faith

Stand for What Is Right Families can be prophetic when they decide to take a stand for what is right. Discuss situations in which you could help create change by speaking the truth—even when it is unpopular. Start by listing your family's values. Place your list where all can see it. Remember: Values are not values unless you practice them.

People of Faith

▲ **John Carroll 1736–1815**

Father **John Carroll**, a friend of Benjamin Franklin, was prophetic. He saw that the needs of Catholics in the colonies in the 1770s were different from those of Catholics in Europe. After the thirteen colonies separated from England, Catholics in the United States wanted a bishop who would live among them. Carroll petitioned the pope for a bishop who would serve the new nation. In 1789 Father Carroll was chosen and was appointed bishop of Baltimore, the center of a diocese that included all of the thirteen colonies.

🌷 Family Prayer

Dear God, lead us to see and respond, as John Carroll did, to the needs in our own communities. Lead us to follow you by helping those we see in need. Amen.

In Unit 3 your child is learning about JESUS CHRIST.

A **Work with Words** Unscramble each of the clue words. Copy the letters in the numbered cells to the empty cells with the same number.

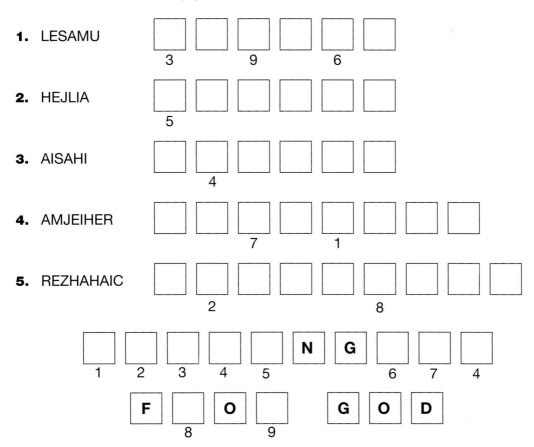

1. LESAMU

☐ ☐ ☐ ☐ ☐ ☐
　3　　　9　　6

2. HEJLIA

☐ ☐ ☐ ☐ ☐ ☐
　5

3. AISAHI

☐ ☐ ☐ ☐ ☐ ☐
　　4

4. AMJEIHER

☐ ☐ ☐ ☐ ☐ ☐ ☐ ☐
　　　7　　1

5. REZHAHAIC

☐ ☐ ☐ ☐ ☐ ☐ ☐ ☐ ☐
　　2　　　　　8

☐ ☐ ☐ ☐ ☐ **N** **G** ☐ ☐ ☐
1　2　3　4　5　　　　6　7　4

F ☐ **O** ☐ 　 **G** **O** **D**
　　8　　9

B **Check Understanding** Match each description in Column 1 with the correct word in Column 2.

Column 1

_____ 6. an understanding of God's purpose and plan

_____ 7. to mark as a sign of God's favor

_____ 8. a messenger from God to the people

_____ 9. poem or hymn used for worshiping God

_____ 10. title meaning "God's anointed"

Column 2

a. prophet

b. messiah

c. psalm

d. wisdom

e. anoint

Unit 4
The Church

In this unit you will...

learn that Jesus founded the Church and built it on Peter and the Apostles. The Church's mission and work is rooted in the gospel, the good news of Jesus' life and teachings. Jesus sent the Holy Spirit to give life to the Church and help us spread the good news. All Church members share the gospel with others and together we become closer to the Triune God.

Chapter 10

Chapter 11

Chapter 12

What do you think you will learn in this unit about the Church's mission?

Chapter 10 Good News

Let Us Pray

Leader: God our Father, thank you for sending Jesus.

"Blessed is he
who comes in the name of the LORD."

Psalm 118:26

All: God our Father, thank you for sending Jesus. Amen.

Activity — Let's Begin

A Ripple Effect   Christina was checking her e-mail when a new message popped up. After reading the message, she called out to her mom, "Aunt Elena had her baby! It's a boy! I have a cousin named Alberto! I'm going to send a message to Grandma right away!"

Good news like Christina's is meant to be shared and spread around. It is like a stone thrown into a quiet pond. Just as the stone causes ripples to radiate across the whole pond, good news spreads and grows through your whole family and community.

• What good news have you shared recently with your family and friends?

Jesus Shares Good News

Focus How did Jesus spread his good news?

Jesus began to share good news as a faithful Jewish boy who knew the Hebrew story of faith. Many years would pass before Jesus would begin his public ministry. But already he had begun to understand that he had a unique role to play. One day, Jesus would be revealed to all of his followers as the Redeemer who would give his life for all.

✝ SCRIPTURE   The Gospel of Luke

In the Temple

When Jesus was twelve, he and his family went to Jerusalem for the feast of Passover. When the customary rituals were completed, the family headed home to Nazareth, but Jesus stayed behind. A day passed before Mary and Joseph realized that he wasn't in the caravan. His parents returned to Jerusalem and found Jesus in the Temple, listening to the teachers and asking questions.

"Son, why have you done this to us?" Mary said to Jesus. "Your father and I have been looking for you with great anxiety."

"Why were you looking for me?" Jesus asked. "Did you not know that I must be in my Father's house?"

Jesus returned with them to Nazareth and was obedient. He grew in age, wisdom, and favor.

Based on *Luke 2:41–52*

❓ **Why did Jesus say that he had to be in his Father's house?**

In the Synagogue

When Jesus was a grown man, he went to the synagogue in Nazareth to read the Scriptures and worship God.

Words of Faith

The **Sabbath** was the seventh day of the week in the Jewish calendar. It is still observed by Jews as a day of rest and prayer and worship.

✝ SCRIPTURE

The Gospel of Luke

The Anointed One

On this **Sabbath**, Jesus was invited to read from the scroll of the prophet Isaiah. He read about the promised one, God's anointed.

> "The Spirit of the Lord is upon me,
>   because he has anointed me
>   to bring glad tidings to the poor.
> He has sent me to proclaim liberty
>   to captives
>   and recovery of sight to the blind,
>   to let the oppressed go free,
> and to proclaim a year acceptable
>   to the Lord."

After reading, Jesus said, "Today this scripture passage is fulfilled in your hearing."

Everyone was amazed. "Isn't this the son of Joseph?" they asked.

Based on *Luke 4:16–22*

Activity — Share Your Faith

Reflect: Imagine that you are one of the people in the synagogue, listening to Jesus.

Share: With a partner, make up an ending for the story that tells what you think the people did in response to Jesus' announcement. Then read *Luke 4:28–30* to find out what really happened.

Act: Write below what you would do in response to Jesus' announcement.

_____

_____

_____

The Gospels

 **Focus** How did Jesus' good news spread after he returned to his Father in heaven?

There were no reporters or historians taking notes when Jesus lived on earth. The words Jesus spoke and the important events of his life were handed down through oral tradition, by word of mouth.

After Jesus' death and Resurrection, the Apostles and other followers of Jesus told people what they had heard and experienced. The stories they told were written down after a time and became the Gospels you read today. The word *gospel* means "good news." The Gospels are part of the **New Testament** of the Bible. They are the foundation of the Church's faith.

THE GOSPELS: WHO, WHEN, WHAT

MARK

The Gospel according to Mark probably came first, before A.D. 72. It is traditionally attributed to John Mark, a companion of Paul and Peter. John Mark starts his Gospel with the ministry of John the Baptist. The Gospel according to Mark is very short, and almost all of what the evangelist wrote is also in the Gospels according to Matthew and Luke.

MATTHEW

The Gospel according to Matthew was written after A.D. 72. This Gospel is named for Matthew, the tax collector who was an Apostle of Jesus. It was written for Jewish Christians and begins with a list of Jesus' ancestors. You will find in Matthew many stories of healing and parables about the kingdom of God.

LUKE

The Gospel according to Luke was also written some time after A.D. 72. The author was probably also a companion of Paul. He wrote for Christians who had not been members of the Jewish religion, and he started his Gospel with the announcement of Jesus' birth. More than half of the Gospel of Luke is unique and not found in the other three Gospels.

JOHN

The Gospel according to John was written near the end of the first century A.D. The author, probably a disciple of the Apostle John, wrote to a community of believers, probably in Asia Minor. This Gospel begins before the creation of the world. The Gospel according to John stands apart from the other three because so much of its content is not found anywhere else. It is a reflection on the meaning of Jesus.

? Why are the Gospels so important to the Church?

The Church and the Gospels

Jesus wanted the good news of salvation to continue to be shared. After Jesus' death and Resurrection, the Holy Spirit moved the Apostles and other followers of Jesus to announce to the world the good news. They proclaimed that Jesus is the Son of the living God who came to establish God's kingdom for all people. The excitement and enthusiasm of Jesus' followers led many people to join them in believing in Jesus. Small communities of prayer and worship started to emerge, and so the **Church** grew.

Over time, many names and images have been used to describe the Church:

- **Assembly.** The Church is an assembly, or convocation. The Church is a worldwide assembly of all those who believe in the good news of Jesus.

- **Sacrament.** The Church is the sacrament of salvation. It proclaims and lives the gospel of Jesus Christ in the world. The Church is the sign and instrument in Christ of the communion of God and humans; it is a visible and effective sign of God's love for the world.

- **Body of Christ.** The Church is the Body of Christ. Christ is the head of the body. Through the Spirit and his actions in the sacraments, Christ establishes the community of believers as his own Body. All members of Christ's Body try to imitate the Jesus of the Gospels as they continue the work of Jesus in the world.

? **What are some other images that describe the Church?**

Words of Faith

The **New Testament** is the second part of the Bible. It is about the story of Jesus, his followers, and the early Church.

The **Church** is the community of all baptized people who believe in God and follow Jesus.

Activity — Connect Your Faith

Describe the Church Look up the Bible passages listed below. Write a description of the image of the Church in each passage. On a separate sheet of paper, design and illustrate a banner using one of the images.

John 10:1–11 _____

_____

John 15:1–10 _____

_____

Revelation 21:2–3 _____

_____

Prayer of Thanksgiving

Let Us Pray

Gather and begin with the Sign of the Cross.

Leader: Listen to the good news of Jesus.

Reader 1: God does not show favoritism, but he welcomes each person from every nation who honors and obeys him.

Reader 2: Jesus is Lord of all, and through him is the good news of peace.

Reader 3: God the Father anointed him with the power of the Holy Spirit to do good and to heal the oppressed.

Reader 4: He died on a cross, so that everyone who believes in him may receive forgiveness and healing.

Based on Acts 10:34–43

Leader: Let us pray.

Bow your heads as the leader prays.

All: **Amen.**

Sing together.

To bring good news to the needy, to make the blind to see, the broken hearts healed again, to set the captive free.

"Good News" © 1993, Howard S. Olson

CHAPTER 10

Review and Apply

Ⓐ Work with Words   Circle the letter of the correct response.

1. After days of searching, Mary and Joseph found Jesus _____.

   a. in Bethlehem   **b.** in the Temple

   c. in the town square

2. Reading from the scroll of Isaiah, Jesus announced that he was _____.

   a. God's anointed   **b.** God's ruler of Israel

   c. God's priest for the Temple

3. There are _____ Gospels in the New Testament.

   a. three   **b.** five

   c. four

4. The Church is a worldwide _____.

   a. building   **b.** assembly

   c. government

5. An image of the Church with Christ at its head is the _____.

   a. assembly   **b.** sacraments

   c. Body of Christ

Ⓑ Check Understanding   In your own words, describe what you believe about the good news of Jesus.

_____

_____

Activity — Live Your Faith

Create a Skit   Work with a partner. Think of a situation in which you could show that you are a member of the Body of Christ. Create a skit to demonstrate the gospel values in the choice you make. Outline your skit here.

Family Faith

Catholics Believe

- The Gospels are called the Good News of Jesus because they proclaim his life and teachings.

- They are interpreted by the Church through Tradition and are the source of our belief.

✝ SCRIPTURE

Read *Mark 8:34–38* to learn more about living the Gospel message.

GO ONLINE www.harcourtreligion.com
For weekly Scripture readings and seasonal resources

Activity
Live Your Faith

Discuss the Readings
Start the tradition of discussing the Sunday readings before or after Mass. You probably can find a list of the next Sunday's readings each week in your parish bulletin. At the end of the week, record in words or pictures the way you have lived this Gospel message during the week. You could create a special notebook, using your family name in the title.

GOOD NEW OF THE FAMILY

People of Faith

John was a relative of Jesus and the son of Elizabeth and Zechariah. John first appears in the Gospel of Mark, preaching and baptizing. He had many followers, but John told his followers that someone more powerful was coming. When Jesus approached him at the River Jordan, John recognized Jesus as the Messiah and granted his request for baptism. John was later executed by the ruler of Galilee. The feast of the birth of John the Baptist is June 24. The passion of John the Baptist is celebrated on August 29.

▲ **Saint John the Baptist**
C. 4 B.C.–A.D. 28

Family Prayer

Saint John the Baptist, pray for us that we may deepen our faith in Jesus and be faithful to our baptismal promises. Amen.

Chapter 11 The Church Begins

Let Us Pray

Leader: Lord God, renew us by your Spirit.

"When you send forth your breath, they are created,
and you renew the face of the earth."

Psalm 104:30

All: Lord God, renew us by your Spirit. Amen.

Activity  Let's Begin

Without a Leader It was the day of the big game. The Hornets had practiced hard and played well all season. Their coach had unified the team and guided it through some pretty rough times. She had been tough but fair, and the whole team had come to trust her leadership.

On the day of the game, everyone was up for the game. Then came the bad news. Coach Mendez had been called out of town for a family emergency. The team would have to play without its leader!

• Choose an ending for the story. What do you think will happen?

The Coming of the Spirit

Focus What happened after Jesus died?

Like a team without its coach, the Apostles did not know what to do after Jesus died. In addition, one of them, Thomas, had a difficult time believing that Jesus had been raised from the dead. The other Apostles had spoken to the Risen Christ and knew his Resurrection to be a true event. It was not until Jesus entered the room without using a door and showed the wounds in his hands and side that "doubting Thomas" came to a fuller faith and realized that Jesus had truly been raised and was alive. (See *John 20:24–29.*) Here is more of Thomas's story.

SCRIPTURE
Acts of the Apostles

After the Resurrection

Many people still call me "doubting Thomas." The last time I saw Jesus was in Jerusalem. He was standing there among us, saying that he would send us the Spirit and that we would be his witnesses to the ends of the earth. And then, suddenly, he was gone; he had returned to his Father in heaven.

We were on our own. The one who had brought us together and given us hope was no longer with us. He was our leader and our strength, and he was gone. Jesus had told us to stay in Jerusalem. Not knowing what else to do, we stayed. And we waited. Since it seemed fitting to replace Judas in order to have twelve Apostles, we elected Matthias. He had been with Jesus ever since John had baptized Jesus at the Jordan River. Mary, Jesus' mother, was also with us. She prayed with us and gave us hope.

Pentecost

When the day of Pentecost arrived, all of us were together in this house. All at once, a wind rose up and shook the house. Something like tongues of fire appeared over our heads. We felt the presence of the Holy Spirit that Jesus had promised. We started talking in many tongues, yet we could still understand one another. We then went outside, where a large crowd had gathered. Now these folks, who had come from all over the world, were staying in Jerusalem. They spoke many different languages, yet they could understand us when we told them about the Risen Jesus and all the things that he had done.

Based on Acts 1:1–26, 2:1–13

? **What effect did the Holy Spirit have on everyone?**

Activity — Share Your Faith

Reflect: Imagine that you are with the disciples on Pentecost. What are your fears and doubts?

Share: Together with two or three other students, list the gifts that the world needs from the Holy Spirit today in order to improve communication between nations.

Act: In the space below, write a petition for one of those gifts. Add the petition to a collage of prayers to the Holy Spirit.

_____

_____

_____

The Church Continues

◎ **Focus** How does the Church carry out its mission?

At Pentecost, the followers of Jesus were excited that they now had a mission. Even though Jesus wasn't physically present, they had his Spirit to guide and inspire them.

The Early Church

The story of the early Church is told in the Acts of the Apostles, the fifth book of the New Testament. Here you read how the Spirit transformed the Apostle Peter, a humble fisher, into a powerful leader. Jesus had called Peter to be one of his first disciples. The special authority that Jesus gave to Peter made this Apostle first among the early leaders in the Church.

Unlike Peter, Paul was not a disciple of Jesus during the time when Jesus physically lived on earth. On the road to Damascus, Paul met the Risen Christ and heard the voice of Jesus. He became a Christian and then a **missionary**, one who is sent to bring good news. Because Paul was chosen by Jesus and experienced the Risen Lord, he too has been called an apostle.

On three journeys through Asia Minor and Greece, Paul proclaimed the gospel to Jews and non-Jews.

❓ **Describe the mission of the early Church. How is it similar to the mission of the Church today?**

Martyrs for the Faith

Many powerful leaders, including Roman emperors, feared the spread of the good news and saw the emerging Christian Church as a threat to their power and influence. When Christians refused to renounce their belief in Jesus, they were often executed for standing up for their beliefs. Called martyrs, they suffered death in witness to their faith in Jesus. Both Peter and Paul were martyred.

The Church Today

The Church today reflects its past. Like the early Christians, Christians today are baptized, and they gather for the Eucharist. They also pray over those who are sick, encourage the confession of sin, and promote faithful marriages. Some even sacrifice their lives as witnesses for Jesus just as the early Christians did.

The Church is built on the lasting foundation of the Apostles. **Apostolic succession** means that the bishops, in a direct line of succession from the Apostles, receive the authority and power of Jesus to lead and teach the Church. Therefore, bishops, united with the pope, share in the mission of the Apostles. The first among the bishops is the pope, who is Peter's successor and the visible head of the Church.

 To what extent are you willing to profess your faith as a Christian openly?

 When is this hardest to do?

Words of Faith

A **missionary** is one who is sent to proclaim the good news of God's kingdom to people in other places or distant lands.

Apostolic succession is the term used to describe how the authority and power to lead and teach the Church is passed down from the Apostles to their successors, the bishops.

Activity — Connect Your Faith

Take a Stand   Imagine that you are among strangers who are making fun of people who believe as you do. In the space at right, describe what you fear might happen if you were to tell these people of your beliefs. Together with your classmates, participate in a short class prayer for courage to stand firm in your faith.

I am afraid they might

_____

_____

_____

_____

_____

_____

Prayer of Petition

Let Us Pray

Gather and begin with the Sign of the Cross.

Leader: Spirit of God, come to our assistance.

All: **Lord, make haste to help us.**

Reader: *Read John 14:23–27.*

Group 1: Come, Holy Spirit, fill the hearts of your faithful, and kindle in us the fire of your love.

Group 2: Send forth your Spirit and we shall be created, and you will renew the face of the earth.

Group 1: Lord, by the light of the Holy Spirit, you have taught the hearts of the faithful.

Group 2: In the same Spirit, help us choose what is right and always rejoice in your consolation.

All: **We ask this through Christ our Lord. Amen.**

Leader: Let us pray.

Bow your heads as the leader prays.

All: **Amen.**

Sing together.

Come Lord Jesus, send us your Spirit,
renew the face of the earth.
Come Lord Jesus, send us your Spirit,
renew the face of the earth.

"Send Us Your Spirit", David Haas, © 1981,
1982, 1987, GIA Publications, Inc.

The Holy Spirit, **The Pierpont Morgan Library**

Review and Apply

Ⓐ Work with Words   Match each description in Column 1 with the correct term in Column 2.

Column 1

_____ **1.** a person who learns from a master

_____ **2.** the first leader of Jesus' disciples

_____ **3.** one sent to proclaim the good news of Jesus

_____ **4.** Acts of the Apostles tells the story

_____ **5.** not a follower of Jesus until after the Resurrection

Column 2

a. first generation of the Church

b. disciple

c. Paul

d. Peter

e. missionary

Ⓑ Check Understanding   Describe what happened to Jesus' followers at Pentecost.

_____

_____

_____

_____

_____

Activity   Live Your Faith

Write What You Believe   When the early Christians witnessed to their faith, they told what they believed. On a card, write a statement of your faith. Tell what you believe about God the Father, Jesus the Son, the Holy Spirit, and the Church. Decorate your card with symbols of your faith in Jesus.

Family Faith

Catholics Believe

- Jesus founded the Church through his life and teachings. He sent the Holy Spirit to help the Church fulfill its mission.

- The Holy Spirit continues to animate the Church today.

✝ SCRIPTURE

Read *Ezekiel 37:1–14* to hear how the Holy Spirit worked in Old Testament times.

www.harcourtreligion.com
For weekly Scripture readings and seasonal resources

Activity
Live Your Faith

Eat and Share Together   Read *Acts of the Apostles 2:42–47* to recall how the early Church community lived. The next time that all family members are able to attend Sunday Mass together, go out for a meal after the Mass, or plan a family meal at home. Discuss the Gospel message you heard at Mass and what it challenges you to do this week. Ask for the blessing of the Holy Spirit on the work of your family.

People of Faith

Matthias had been with the followers of Jesus from the time when John was baptizing. He was a witness to Jesus' Resurrection and his Ascension to the right hand of the Father. After the Apostle Judas betrayed Jesus and died, the rest of the Apostles met together in Jerusalem to replace him. They prayed and then cast lots to choose a successor. Matthias was chosen. From then on, he was one of the Twelve Apostles. Matthias may have preached in Greece, and he died a martyr. His feast day is May 14.

▲ Saint Matthias
c. first century

🙌 Family Prayer

Saint Matthias, pray for us that we may be Jesus' witnesses to the world in everything we do. May our words and actions be pleasing to God. Amen.

The Church Community

Let Us Pray

Leader: Merciful God, keep us in your tender care.

"For this is our God,
whose people we are,
God's well-tended flock."

Psalm 95:7

All: Merciful God, keep us in your tender care. Amen.

Activity — Let's Begin

Keep in Touch "My friend Quentin is moving all the way across the country," said Trevor. "I might never see him again."

"That's too bad," said Trevor's mom. "But you know that your Aunt Polly lives in Australia, and we still keep in touch with her. We even see her every few years."

"Every few years!" Trevor groaned. But then he thought it over. "I guess I could write long letters, the way you do."

"Even short notes or postcards make me smile," his mom said. "And you can send photos, too."

"I can e-mail him, too. And maybe I can visit him. I've never been out West before."

• Who is someone you keep in touch with regularly?

• What are your main ways of communicating with friends or family members who don't live near you?

Keeping in Touch

Focus What do the Letters of the New Testament tell you?

Letters have for centuries been an important way to communicate with others. Several letters are included in the Bible. Letters may offer both information and instruction to those who receive them.

A STORY

The Letter Writer

Like Trevor, who wanted to stay in touch with his friend, a twelve-year-old Jewish girl named Rifka stayed in touch with family members by writing letters. Rifka's family emigrated from Russia to the United States in 1919 to find religious freedom.

Before Rifka left Russia, her cousin Tovah had given her a book of poetry. Rifka knew that she would probably never see her cousin again. With her cousin in mind, Rifka wrote letters that she could not send. Writing on the blank pages and in the margins of the poetry book, she shared with Tovah her sense of loss, her trials, her joys, and her fears. She related her heartbreak at temporarily being rejected for travel because of a contagious disease and of being separated from her family, and she eventually wrote about her journey to the United States.

Finally, when Rifka was reunited with her family, she wrote this letter to Tovah.

❓ **Why do you think Rifka wanted so much to express her thoughts and feelings to her cousin Tovah?**

"I will write to you tonight a real letter, a letter I can send. I will wrap up our precious book and send it to you, too, so that you will know of my journey. I hope you can read all the words I squeezed onto the worn pages. I hope they bring to you the comfort they have brought to me. At last I send you my love from America."

136

Letters of the New Testament

In the days of the early Church two thousand years ago, communicating long distance was not that much different from communicating in Rifka's time. The Apostles and many disciples took long journeys to spread the word about Jesus, and they started many new Christian communities. When they moved on, many of these disciples wrote letters, or **epistles**, to the new groups. God spoke through these letters, and many of them are now part of the New Testament. The letters with the names of Paul, Peter, James, John, and Jude tell the story of how the Apostles and disciples planted the seeds of Christianity.

The **epistles**, or letters, were written by Paul and several of the other Apostles and disciples to new Christian communities that they established. There are twenty-one letters in the New Testament.

The First Letter to the Thessalonians

Rejoice always. Pray without ceasing. In all circumstances give thanks, for this is the will of God for you in Christ Jesus.

1 Thessalonians 5:16–18

The First Letter of Peter

As each one has received a gift, use it to serve one another as good stewards of God's varied grace.

1 Peter 4:10

The Letter of James

For just as a body without a spirit is dead, so also faith without works is dead.

James 2:26

The First Letter of John

Beloved, let us love one another, because love is of God; everyone who loves is begotten by God and knows God.

1 John 4:7

Activity — Share Your Faith

Reflect: Reread the passages above, and choose your favorite.

Share: Share your favorite passage with one other student.

Act: Decide on one action you will take this week that is based on your favorite passage, and write it in the space provided.

_____

_____

_____

_____

Marks of the Church

◎ Focus What do the marks of the Church mean?

The Letters of the New Testament show that the Church is one, holy, catholic, and apostolic. These four characteristics are the **marks of the Church** that have identified the Church from its beginning. In the Nicene **Creed**, the statement of belief that you profess at Mass, you proclaim the four marks of the Church.

One

✝ SCRIPTURE

"As a body is one though it has many parts, and all the parts of the body, though many, are one body, so also Christ."

1 Corinthians 12:12

Paul taught that the faithful are like many parts of one body, with Jesus as the head. Each part relies on the other parts to work well together. Paul is telling you that even though people are different, all can work together in unity as the Body of Christ. In fact, the Church is made up of many different people from all over the world who acknowledge one Lord, confess one faith, celebrate one Baptism.

❷ What is your role in the Church right now?

Holy

✝ SCRIPTURE

"Do you not know that you are the temple of God, and that the Spirit of God dwells in you?"

1 Corinthians 3:16

The presence of the Holy Spirit and the love of Christ make the Church holy. The Spirit fills the Body of Christ, giving the Church life and uniting its members. Thus the Church is called the Temple of the Holy Spirit. The presence of God's Spirit in each person doesn't mean that members of the Church are not sinners. Members of the Church can avoid sin with the help of the Holy Spirit who dwells within them or, if they sin, can accept the divine forgiveness available through the Church.

❷ What does knowing that the Spirit dwells in you challenge you to do?

Faith Fact

Although the Nicene Creed we profess today is named for the Council of Nicaea in A.D. 325, it was actually affirmed at the Council of Constantinople 56 years later.

Catholic

"And [God] put all things beneath [Christ's] feet and gave him as head over all things to the church, which is his body, the fullness of the one who fills all things in every way."

Ephesians 1:22–23

The word *catholic* means universal. The Church is catholic because through Christ it proclaims the fullness of faith and provides everything you need for salvation. Its mission is to all people of the world.

❓ What does it mean to say that the Church has the fullness of salvation for all?

Apostolic

✚ SCRIPTURE

"So then you are no longer strangers and sojourners, but you are fellow citizens with holy ones and members of the household of God, built upon the foundation of the apostles and prophets, with Christ Jesus himself as the capstone."

Ephesians 2:19–20

The Church has faithfully handed on from one generation to the next the teachings that the Apostles learned from Jesus. The Apostles also handed on their authority and mission to others.

❓ What is the source of the Church's authority?

Words of Faith

The **marks of the Church** are the essential characteristics that distinguish the Church and its mission. The Church is one, holy, catholic, and apostolic.

A **creed** is a formal statement of what is believed. The word *creed* comes from the Latin for "I believe." There are two main creeds of the Church: the Nicene Creed and the Apostles' Creed.

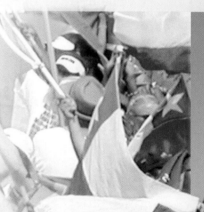

Activity — Connect Your Faith

Read *1 Thessalonians 5:12–22* Imagine that Paul has written one of the messages in this chapter to your class. Answer him below, and tell him how the class has been following his requests.

Dear Paul,

Your Friend,

Celebration of the Word

Let Us Pray

Gather and begin with the Sign of the Cross.

Sing together.

There is one Lord, one faith, one baptism,
There is one God who is Father of all.

"There Is One Lord" © 1984, Les Presses de Taizé, GIA Publications, Inc., agent

Leader:	Joined together as one community, we are called to one faith.
Reader:	A reading from the Letter to the Ephesians.
	Read Ephesians 4:1–6.
	The word of the Lord.
All:	**Thanks be to God.**
Leader:	Let us renew the faith of our Baptism.
	Do you believe in God the Father?
All:	**We do.**
Leader:	Do you believe in Jesus Christ, his only Son?
All:	**We do.**
Leader:	Do you believe in the Holy Spirit, the Lord and giver of life?
All:	**We do.**
Leader:	Let us pray.
	Bow your heads as the leader prays.
All:	**Amen.**

Review and Apply

A **Work with Words**   Complete each sentence with the correct word from the Word Bank.

WORD BANK

apostolic
belief
Letters
Christ
universal
laws
Spirit

1. The four marks of the Church indicate that it is one, holy, catholic, and _____.

2. Paul taught that the faithful are like many parts of one body, with _____ as the head.

3. The word *catholic* means _____.

4. New Testament _____ were written to tell Christian communities how to follow Jesus.

5. A creed is a statement of _____.

B **Check Understanding**   Choose one of the marks of the Church. Give evidence that this mark is in the Church today.

_____

_____

_____

_____

Activity   Live Your Faith

Design a Mosaic   Work with a partner or a small group. Design a mosaic with a scene that reflects one of the beliefs expressed in the Nicene Creed.

Family Faith

◎ Catholics Believe

- The Church is one, holy, catholic, and apostolic.

- The Church is a community of people, united in faith, working together to share the Gospel and become closer to God.

✝ SCRIPTURE

Read *Ephesians 4:1–16* for Paul's recipe for a Church.

GO ONLINE www.harcourtreligion.com
For weekly Scripture readings and seasonal resources

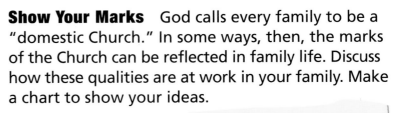

Activity

Live Your Faith

Show Your Marks God calls every family to be a "domestic Church." In some ways, then, the marks of the Church can be reflected in family life. Discuss how these qualities are at work in your family. Make a chart to show your ideas.

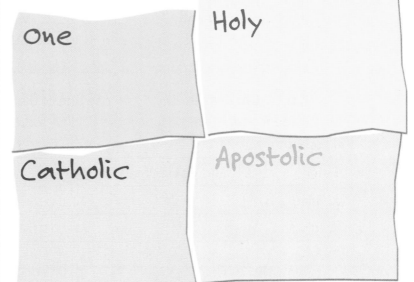

One

Holy

Catholic

Apostolic

People of Faith

▲ The Women Martyrs of El Salvador d. 1980

Jean Donovan, a lay missionary, and **Sisters Dorothy Kazel, Ita Ford,** and **Maura Clarke** were serving as missionaries in El Salvador in 1980. They were working on behalf of the Archdiocese of San Salvador, helping refugees flee the violence of war. As they were leaving the airport in San Salvador, members of the National Guard intercepted their van. The women were taken to an isolated spot, where they were murdered. Their deaths drew worldwide attention to a movement for social justice in Central America that continues today.

🌸 Family Prayer

Dear God, be with us so that we may devote ourselves to sharing the good news with others in what we say and do in our daily lives. Give us your grace. Amen.

UNIT 4 REVIEW

A **Work with Words** Circle the letter of the choice that best completes the sentence.

1. A letter in the New Testament written by Paul or another Apostle is called _____.

    a. an epistle
    b. a psalm
    c. a hymn
    d. a Gospel

2. The four marks of the Church are one, _____, catholic, and apostolic.

    a. loving
    b. faithful
    c. holy
    d. righteous

3. _____ is the seventh day of the week in the Jewish calendar.

    a. Sunday
    b. Friday
    c. The Sabbath
    d. Purim

4. A formal statement of what is believed is called a _____.

    a. testimony
    b. witness
    c. letter
    d. creed

5. Peter's sucessor and visible head of the Church is the _____.

    a. king
    b. pope
    c. disciple
    d. priest

6. The Gospel that begins with the creation of the world is _____.

    a. the Gospel according to Matthew
    b. the Gospel according to Mark
    c. the Gospel according to Luke
    d. the Gospel according to John

7. The New Testament is about the story of Jesus, his followers, and _____.

    a. the last days
    b. the early Church
    c. his enemies
    d. science

8. The one image that is *not* used to describe the Church is _____.

    a. a chariot
    b. the Body of Christ
    c. an assembly
    d. a sacrament

9. Paul was on the road to _____ when he met the Risen Christ.

    a. Jerusalem
    b. Rome
    c. Damascus
    d. Nazareth

10. The phrase "faith without works is dead" is found in _____.

    a. The First Letter of John
    b. The First Letter to the Thessalonians
    c. The First Letter of Peter
    d. The Letter of James

Unit 5
Morality

In this unit you will...

learn that Catholic morality is based on the Great Commandment. Justice means respecting the dignity of all, and it is the foundation for peace. Sin disrupts relationships. Our conscience helps us to know what is right and wrong, and to know when we have sinned or been unjust. We accept God's forgiveness through sincere sorrow. The Sacrament of Reconciliation is a special sacrament of forgiveness.

Chapter
13

Chapter
14

Chapter
15

What do you think you will learn in this unit about the moral life?

Chapter 13 The Law of Love

 **Let Us Pray**

Leader: God, help me obey your law of love.

"To do your will is my delight;
my God, your law is in my heart!"

Psalm 40:9

All: God, help me obey your law of love. Amen.

 **Activity** Let's Begin

A Mitzvah "You're twelve now, Benjamin," his mother said proudly. "Soon it will be time for your *bar mitzvah*."

"I'm ready now," Benjamin told his mother. "I know the commandments of the Law, all the *mitzvoth*."

"But there is more to being a child of the Law than just obeying the laws," Benjamin's mother replied. She reminded her son that he must do a *mitzvah*, a good deed, every day.

• What good deed have you done today?

Old Law and New Law

◎ Focus What is the new law?

A *bar mitzvah,* or *bas mitzvah* for girls, is a religious ceremony for Jewish youth. It takes place at about age thirteen, when these young people take on the adult duties of the Jewish faith. The term *bar* (or *bas*) *mitzvah* means "son (or daughter) of the commandment." Before his thirteenth birthday, Benjamin studied the laws of his faith and learned more about God's everlasting covenant with the Jewish people.

Christians believe that the Law of the Old Testament was the first step and a preparation for the new law of love that would be revealed by Jesus. The Old Law is summed up in the Ten Commandments. These Commandments are just as important for you to follow as they are for Benjamin. Because they are the word of God, they will endure forever.

The great prophets of Israel, such as Isaiah and Jeremiah, tried to call the people back to the wisdom of God's Law and remind them of God's covenant of love with them. God revealed through the prophets that a new day would come when the Law would be fulfilled. This is how God spoke through the prophet Jeremiah.

✝ SCRIPTURE

"But this is the covenant which I will make with the house of Israel after those days, says the LORD. I will place my law within them, and write it upon their hearts; I will be their God, and they shall be my people. No longer will they have need to teach their friends and kinsmen how to know the LORD. All, from least to greatest, shall know me, says the LORD, for I will forgive their evildoing and remember their sin no more."

Jeremiah 31:33–34

❓ **What does it mean to have the law written in your heart?**

❓ **What law is written in your heart that you must always follow?**

The Law Fulfilled

The people of Israel followed the Law of Moses, which included the Ten Commandments and a number of other regulations. When Jesus came, he interpreted the Law in a new way.

Words of Faith

The **transfiguration** is the revelation of Jesus in glory to the Apostles Peter, James, and John.

✝ SCRIPTURE   The Gospel of Matthew

The Transfiguration

One day, Jesus invited Peter, James, and John to pray with him on a high mountain. While Jesus prayed, he suddenly became radiant with light. Moses and Elijah appeared and spoke with him. A voice from heaven said, "This is my beloved Son, with whom I am well pleased; listen to him." The disciples were frightened, but Jesus reassured them.

Based on *Matthew 17:1–8*

This event is known as the **transfiguration**, in which Jesus was revealed as the fulfillment of the Law, represented by Moses, and of the prophets, represented by Elijah. God also showed that he had given his Son authority and that Jesus' words are true forever.

The Transfiguration–Raffaello Sanzio

Activity Share Your Faith

Reflect: Think about a scenario that puts a person in a situation in which he or she must take a stand.

Share: With a small group, share your scenario.

Act: Choose one of the scenarios, and create a skit showing how the person acted from the law in his or her heart.

Jesus' New Message

◎ Focus How does Jesus call you to live?

The Pharisees once asked Jesus which commandment was the greatest. Jesus responded with a simple answer. His reply combines two teachings found in the Old Law.

✝ **SCRIPTURE**

"You shall love the Lord, your God, with all your heart, with all your soul, and with all your mind. This is the greatest and the first commandment. The second is like it: You shall love your neighbor as yourself. The whole law and the prophets depend on these two commandments."

Matthew 22:37–40

Jesus told his followers that he did not come to change the Law of Moses, but to fulfill it. His words and the authority with which he spoke stirred up a great deal of interest.

The Beatitudes

Jesus' teachings about those who are blessed are called the Beatitudes. The Beatitudes are more than commandments or laws; they are a call to a holy way of life, a sign of God's kingdom, and a source of hope.

As often happens today, many people in Jesus' day equated happiness with trouble-free lives, security, and wealth. Jesus calls you to a form of happiness that is greater than any happiness that material things can give. To help you follow this path, the Holy Spirit empowers you with a willing heart, self-discipline, the strength to pray, and the courage to keep your eyes focused on God.

❓ Who around you needs to know God's blessing through your actions?

Freedom to Love

The new law that Jesus brings is a law of freedom. It sets you free to love God and others—to follow the law of love.

The virtue of **charity** is a gift of the Holy Spirit, prompting you to live with love toward all. Charity allows you to show God's love to those who need it most—children, those who are poor and in need, and even your enemies. Charity is the only way of life for a Christian.

❓ **What is another law of God that is rooted in love?**

The Church's Precepts

The Church offers you practical guidance for living a moral life. The **precepts of the Church**, for example, describe some of the important duties of Catholics. They can help you grow in your love of God and neighbor. The precepts are listed in your Catholic Source Book.

All of the Church's precepts are rooted in the love of Christ. As you practice living the Beatitudes and strengthening yourself through the Spirit's gift of charity, you will find yourself living the Church's precepts out of love, rather than from a sense of duty.

Words of Faith

Charity is the theological virtue of loving God above all things and loving your neighbor as yourself for the love of God.

The **precepts of the Church** are the laws given by Church authorities. They are the basic guidelines for spiritual growth.

Activity — Connect Your Faith

Tell About a Christ-like Person   Think of a person you know or have read about who is a good example of the life of a true Christian. Create a word map telling all the Christ-like qualities of this person.

149

Prayer of Praise

 Let Us Pray

Gather and begin with the Sign of the Cross.

Leader: Jesus, you are the Messiah, the one who fulfills the Law as foretold by the prophets.

Sing together.

Jesus Christ, Jesus Christ,
yesterday, today and for ever.

"Jesus Christ, Yesterday, Today and for Ever", Suzanne Toolan, © 1988, GIA Publications, Inc.

Reader: A reading from the holy Gospel according to Mark.

Read Mark 9:2–10.
The Gospel of the Lord.

All: **Praise to you, Lord Jesus Christ.**

Leader: Let us pray.

Side 1: Jesus, you are the new Moses. Help us follow your law of love in our words and actions.

Side 2: Jesus, you fulfill the promises of the ancient prophets. Be with us as we speak out against injustice.

Side 1: Jesus, you promised us the Holy Spirit as our lifelong traveling companion. Help us always turn to the Holy Spirit when we need guidance and when we make decisions.

Side 2: Jesus, you are the way, the truth, and the life. May we always turn to you on our journey, and speak and witness to your truth.

Leader: Let us pray.

Bow your heads as the leader prays.

All: **Amen.**

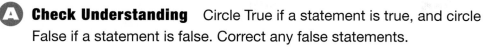
A **Check Understanding**   Circle True if a statement is true, and circle False if a statement is false. Correct any false statements.

1. Jesus' words about love mean you should love even your enemies.

   True   False   _____

2. Following rules is at the heart of the law of love.

   True   False   _____

3. The Beatitudes are more than laws; they are a call to a way of life and a source of hope in difficult times.

   True   False   _____

4. The Sermon on the Mount is the revelation of Jesus in glory to the Apostles Peter, James, and John.

   True   False   _____

5. The precepts of the Church are statements of duties meant to help you grow in the love of God and neighbor as members of the Church.

   True   False   _____

B **Make Connections**   Write one of the Beatitudes. Explain what it means, and give an example of how you can live it today.

_____

_____

_____

Activity   Live Your Faith

Follow the Example   Think of the person whom you chose for your word map in the activity on page 149. Recall some specific actions of this person. Choose a way that you will try to follow the person's example this week. Write your idea here.

_____

_____

_____

Family Faith

Catholics Believe

- **The Great Commandment of Jesus allows you to achieve happiness and holiness.**

- **The Beatitudes and the precepts of the Church help the faithful live holy and dutiful lives.**

✝ SCRIPTURE

Read *Ecclesiastes 4:7–12* to see the benefits of loving your neighbor.

GO ONLINE **www.harcourtreligion.com**
For weekly Scripture readings and seasonal resources

Activity

Live Your Faith

Live the Great Commandment How do the events of daily life reflect your family's commitment to the Great Commandment? List the main events of the past week. Did your family members handle each of them in a way that demonstrates the law of love? Rate your overall performance on a scale from one to ten.

People of Faith

▲ **Blessed Dorothy Chavez Orozco 1867–1949**

Dorothy was born in Mexico. She was known for her devotion to the Infant Jesus. In 1892 when Dorothy became ill, she was inspired to dedicate her life to God by helping those who were poor and sick. In 1905 she founded the Servants of the Holy Trinity and the Poor. She was named Superior General in 1913, a position she held for thirty years. The Servants cared for the wounded during the Mexican Revolution and opened seventeen hospitals, clinics, and nurseries. Dorothy was beatified in November 1997. Her feast day is July 19.

🌸 Family Prayer

Merciful God, help us follow the example of Blessed Dorothy by showing compassion to those who are poor and sick and by remaining faithful to the law of love, even during difficult times. Amen.

In Unit 5 your child is learning about MORALITY.

Chapter 14 Justice and Peace

Let Us Pray

Leader: Lord God, help us demonstrate your justice.

"See how I long for your precepts;
in your justice give me life."

Psalm 119:40

All: Lord God, help us demonstrate your justice. Amen.

Activity — Let's Begin

What Is Success?

What is success?
To laugh often and love much;
To win the respect of intelligent people
and the affection of children;
To earn the appreciation of honest critics
and endure the betrayal of false friends;
To appreciate beauty;
To find the best in others;
To leave the world a bit better, whether by
a healthy child, a garden patch,
or a redeemed social condition;
To know even one life has breathed
easier because you have lived;
This is to have succeeded.

Excerpts from the poem by Bessie Stanley

• What does success mean to you?

Seeking Justice

Focus What does it mean to act justly?

Sometimes bringing justice and peace may appear to lead to failure rather than to success.

A STORY

Injustice

Once there was a city called Injustice. It was ruled by cheaters and liars, who felt no pity for others and laughed at their suffering. One day a stranger came to Injustice. Nobody paid much attention to him at first. He gathered the children together and told them stories about a place called Justice. Everyone there was happy, safe, and at peace. All had what they needed. Those who were sick, poor, or old were cared for. The rulers of Justice led the people by serving them.

The Tree of Life, John August S...

As the people listened to the stories about Justice, they were more and more eager to go there to live. Some asked where Justice was. The stranger replied, "It is as near as your heart."

The leaders of Injustice grew angry and worried as they listened to the stranger. They decided to kill him in front of the people. Then everyone would forget about Justice. So the leaders held a trial and condemned the stranger. As the people watched and wept, their hero was executed before their eyes. Of all the sad days in Injustice, this was the saddest.

The good people sighed when they remembered the stranger's stories of Justice. He had given them a glimmer of hope. Now, it seemed, they would never get to Justice. Then one child spoke up. "Don't worry," she said. "We don't have to go anywhere to get Justice. We can make a place called Justice. We can build it in our hearts."

❓ **Why do you think the leaders of Injustice feared the stranger so much?**

God's Law

The child in the story spoke wisely when she said that justice is built in people's hearts. The search for justice is a response to the natural moral law, the understanding that God places in every human.

The natural moral law expresses the God-given **dignity**, or inner worth, of all persons. Anything that robs you or others of that dignity is unjust. Classmates, family members, enemies, people who live in other lands, people who are poor, criminals locked away in prison—all are humans with God-given dignity.

Justice means giving God and other people what is due to them. It is a virtue or habit of goodness that helps you grow in love for God and others.

God's grace helps you live a virtuous life. The Ten Commandments, the Beatitudes, and the law of love help you understand how to act justly.

Yet there are those who disobey God's law and ignore Jesus' example of loving others. As a consequence, many people still suffer injustice.

Words of Faith

Dignity is the inner worth of persons because they are made in the image and likeness of God.

Justice means giving God what is due him. It also means giving each person what he or she is due because that person is a child of God.

Activity — Share Your Faith

Reflect: Think about an unjust action that you have witnessed or experienced.

Share: With a partner, brainstorm when or why actions are unjust.

Act: Write two sentences about the unjust action that you witnessed or experienced. State why it was unjust and how the act made you feel.

_____

_____

_____

_____

155

Peace

◎ Focus What is the relationship between peace and justice?

Where there is an absence of justice, there is no **peace**. Only people and nations who live in justice will know real peace.

The Law addressed issues of peace and justice among the Israelites, such as paying workers their wages on time. But not everyone listened. About eight centuries before Christ, three prophets spoke of people living without justice and peace. God said through the prophets that the people would bear the consequences of their sin, but that God would never stop loving them.

Three Prophets

Hosea reported that lying, murder, stealing, and adultery had replaced fidelity and mercy. Yet he prophesied that one day God would heal the sinners and love them freely. "I will be like the dew of Israel: he shall blossom like the lily … ." (Hosea 14:6).

Amos observed that the weak were trampled down, that the just were oppressed, and that bribery was everywhere. Yet Amos also pointed out that one day God would restore his people, Israel, and return them to their land. The prophet Micah reminded people that the path to righteousness was simple.

✝ SCRIPTURE

"You have been told, O man, what is good,
  and what the LORD requires of you:

Only to do the right and to love goodness,
  and to walk humbly with your God."

Micah 6:8

❓ Who needs to hear the message of these three prophets today?

Faith Fact

There are three theological virtues—faith, hope, and love—and four cardinal virtues—prudence, justice, fortitude, and temperance.

Justice Seekers and Peacemakers

Today the Church continues the work of the Old Testament prophets. The Church helps you understand the responsibility you have to work for justice and peace as Jesus did. There are certain areas that need your close attention.

- **Dignity.** Your duty as a Christian citizen is to work with those in authority to build a society in which the dignity of all people is respected. Christians must work to reject and counteract prejudice and discrimination.

- **Life.** Your duty is to protect all human life and work for peace, striving to heal injustices that threaten human life.

- **Basic needs.** Your duty is to care for those who are poor and to see that they have adequate food, shelter, and clothing.

Social Sin

The failure to give others what is due them is an injustice. When personal sin leads whole communities or societies to make such choices, the sin grows. This kind of sin can be called **social sin**. Racism, sexism, and terrorism are examples of social sins.

You are part of a tradition of Catholic social teaching that promotes justice and peace. Pope Paul VI wrote about the relationship between justice and peace. He said, "Peace is more than the absence of war." He also said, "If you want peace, work for justice." Wherever there is hatred, envy, prejudice, or division between people, there is no real peace. A just world is a sign of the kingdom of God.

© Harcourt Religion

Words of Faith

Peace is the state of tranquillity or harmony in which people respect the dignity of others.

Social sin refers to unjust structures that can occur as the result of personal sin. One person's sin can cause others to sin, and the sin can spread through a whole society.

Activity Connect Your Faith

Be a Filmmaker You are a film director on a film about peacemakers. Plan the film. Who will be in it? What is the problem? How will it be resolved?

_____

_____

_____

_____

Prayer of Lament

Let Us Pray

Gather and begin with the Sign of the Cross.

Reader 1: He was spurned and avoided by men,
  a man of suffering, accustomed to infirmity,
One of those from whom men hide their faces,
  spurned, and we held him in no esteem.

Reader 2: Yet it was our infirmities that he bore,
  our sufferings that he endured,
While we thought of him as stricken,
  as one smitten by God and afflicted.

Reader 3: Oppressed and condemned, he was taken away,
  and who would have thought any more of
    his destiny?

Reader 4: Through his suffering, my servant
  shall justify many,
  and their guilt he shall bear . . .

Reader 5: Because he surrendered himself to death
  and was counted among the wicked;
And he shall take away the sins of many,
  and win pardon for their offenses.

Isaiah 53:3–4, 8, 11–12

All: **Amen.**

Sing together.

We are called to act with justice, we are called to love tenderly,
we are called to serve one another; to walk humbly with God!

"We Are Called", David Haas, © 1988, GIA Publications, Inc.

A **Work with Words**   Complete the following statements.

1. Where there is an absence of justice, there is no

   _____.

2. The Church teaches you the language of _____.

3. The prophet _____ called the people to do the right thing, love goodness, and walk humbly with God.

4. Pope Paul VI said, "If you want peace, work for

   _____."

5. _____ is the inner worth of all people, because all are made in the image of God.

B **Check Understanding**   What is social sin? Give two examples.

_____

_____

_____

_____

_____

Activity Live Your Faith

Create a Commercial   Create a public service commercial for television that reminds people of their responsibility to bring justice into the world. Remember to express your message in very few words and in language that will catch the attention of the viewer. Present your commercial to the class.

Family Faith

◎ Catholics Believe

■ Working toward justice means respecting the dignity of persons and peoples.

■ Justice is giving what is due to God and others. Where justice is absent, peace is not possible.

✝ SCRIPTURE

Read *Proverbs 24:23–29* to learn how you can treat others with the respect and dignity they deserve.

GO
ONLINE
www.harcourtreligion.com
For weekly Scripture readings and seasonal resources

Activity
Live Your Faith

Promote Human Dignity Here are some ways of promoting human dignity. Discuss how your family can carry out each suggestion.

1. Look for the presence of Jesus in everyone.
2. Be honest with others.
3. Avoid stereotyping and prejudice.
4. Stand up for the rights of others.
5. Avoid items and messages that insult human dignity.

People of Faith

John came from a wealthy French family, but he gave his life and his wealth to educating children who were poor. He founded the Christian Brothers to open educational opportunities to boys. Because the Brothers' mission was to pass on the faith, John instructed them to read from the New Testament every day. Later, he founded the first training college for teachers. The Brothers of the Christian Schools continue Saint John's work today. His feast day is April 7.

▲ **Saint John Baptist de la Salle 1651–1719**

🌸 Family Prayer

Saint John, pray for us that we may be brothers and sisters to all those who are poor. May we do what we can to help them. Amen.

In Unit 5 your child is learning about MORALITY.

Chapter 15 Sin and Forgiveness

Let Us Pray

Leader: Gracious God, thank you for your forgiveness.

"Deliver us, pardon our sins
for your name's sake."

Psalm 79:9

All: Gracious God, thank you for your forgiveness. Amen.

Activity — Let's Begin

When I Die (Part II)

When I die, I want to be
A child in Heaven.
I want to be
A ten-year-old cherub.
I want to be
A hero in Heaven
Just like my goal on earth.
I will ask God if I can
Help the people in purgatory
I will help them think,
About their life,
About their spirits,
About their future.
I will help them
Hear their Heartsongs again,
So they can finally
See the face of God.
So soon,
When I die,
I want to be,
Just like I want to be
Here on earth.

An excerpt from the poem by Mattie Stepanek,
November 1999

• Mattie's heartsong is about peace. He believes it is his life's work. What heartsong do you hear deep in your heart?

Your Relationship with God

Focus What does Jesus teach about sin and forgiveness?

Mattie Stepanek's greatest concern in life is to help others restore the peace that has been lost by the presence of sin in the world. Sin disrupts the harmony of God's plan for creation. It also affects your relationship with God and others.

Sin can be serious (mortal) or less serious (venial). **Mortal sin** is a deliberate and freely chosen act. It is a very serious sin that turns someone completely away from God. The primary reason for the Sacrament of Reconciliation is the confession and forgiveness of mortal sins. If left unrepented, mortal sin puts a person in danger of hell after death.

The sacrament is also a means of healing for those who have fallen into less serious sin. Venial sins are less serious sins that weaken but do not destroy your relationship with God. Deliberate venial sins for which you are not sorry can move you gradually toward a decision to commit mortal sin.

? How could a venial sin lead to more serious sin?

Words of Faith

Mortal sin is a very serious sin that turns someone completely away from God. The conditions of mortal sin are these:

1. The matter must be serious.
2. The person must know that the action is serious and sinful.
3. The person must freely choose to do the sinful action.

God's Mercy

In the parable of the unforgiving servant, Jesus teaches an important lesson about God's mercy and forgiveness.

The Unforgiving Servant

There once was a king who decided to settle accounts with his servants. One servant owed him a huge amount. The king ordered the man to be sold, along with his family and possessions, in payment of his debt. Hearing this, the servant begged the king's mercy and the king forgave him his debt.

The forgiven debtor then found a fellow servant who owed him a much smaller amount. He demanded that the other man pay everything he owed. The fellow servant fell to his knees and begged for mercy. Instead of finding mercy, the man was thrown into jail until he paid the debt.

When the king found out about the incident, he said to the forgiven debtor, "I forgave you your entire debt because you begged me to. Should you not have had pity on your fellow servant, as I had pity on you?" Then the king sent the debtor to prison until he paid back what he owed.

Jesus then said to his disciples, "So will my heavenly Father do to you, unless each of you forgives his brother from his heart."

Based on *Matthew 18:23–35*

Activity — Share Your Faith

Reflect: Think about someone who needs your forgiveness.

Share: With a partner, list ways of showing forgiveness to others.

_____

_____

_____

Act: Decide how you will forgive a person who needs your forgiveness.

163

Making Things Right

◎ Focus How can you inform your conscience?

The Man at the Fruit Stand

A group of girls and boys went to a Saturday afternoon game. Their parents expected them home in time for dinner. The game ran into overtime, and the kids had to run to catch the bus. In the rush, one of the boys accidentally kicked over a basket of apples at a fruit stand. Without stopping, the group reached the bus–all but one boy. He waved good-bye to the group and returned to the fruit stand. He was especially glad that he did. The man selling the apples was blind.

❓ **What choices did the characters face?**

❓ **What were the results of their choices?**

❓ **What would you have done?**

❓ **What teaching of Jesus could have helped the girls and boys choose?**

Conscience

The boy who stopped to help heard an interior voice that prompted him to think of others.

In your heart God has written an inner law that you can use to help you recognize good and evil. Your **conscience** is like an interior voice that acts as a wise adviser, an adviser who prompts you by saying, "Do this" or "Don't do that." Your conscience is your free will and right reason, or good sense, working together to help you make good choices. You should always obey the certain judgment of an informed conscience.

Your informed conscience is like a fine tool. It is meant to be maintained and used. You maintain it by listening with your mind and heart to the word of God in the Bible, the teaching of the Church, the good advice of wise people, and the prompting of the ever-present Holy Spirit.

164

The Sacrament of Reconciliation

When you sin, the Church provides a way for you to experience God's forgiveness through the Sacrament of Reconciliation, or Penance. Here are the steps you take to celebrate the sacrament.

- Carefully examine your conscience, deciding in what ways you have failed to love God and others.
- Confess any unconfessed mortal sins to a priest. The Church encourages you to confess your venial sins also.
- Pray an Act of Contrition to express your sorrow for sin and your intention to avoid sin.
- Receive the forgiveness or absolution from the priest.
- Perform the penance the priest gives you to make up for your sins.

Effects of the Sacrament

The Sacrament of Reconciliation provides you with many benefits. Your full friendship with God is restored or healed. You are reconciled with the Church and freed from the threat of hell. You are given peace and strength to do what is right and good. Any sin confessed in the sacrament can never be told to anyone by the priest. This is called the sacramental seal, or seal of confession.

Words of Faith

Conscience is a gift from God that helps you know the difference between right and wrong and helps you choose what is right.

The **sacramental seal** refers to the rule that a priest may not reveal anything that he hears in confession.

Activity — Connect Your Faith

Express Your View Circle the words or phrases that best express your feelings about the Sacrament of Reconciliation:

relief	cleaning up	God	end of hurting
healing	grace	return	making amends
peace	friendship	starting over	freedom

Add words or phrases of your own.

_____

_____

_____

Prayer of Petition

Let Us Pray

Gather and begin with the Sign of the Cross.

Place yourself in a position of prayer, and breathe deeply and quietly. Now combine your focused breathing with an ancient prayer.

All: *As you breathe in, silently pray,* **Lord Jesus Christ.**
As you breathe out, silently pray, **Son of God.**
As you breathe in, silently pray, **have mercy on me.**
As you breathe out, silently pray, **a sinner.**

All: **God our Father, you do not want to lose anyone to sin. Help us do good and avoid evil. If we fail, guide us to your forgiveness in the Sacrament of Reconciliation. We ask this through Jesus, your Son, who lives and reigns with you and the Holy Spirit now and forever. Amen.**

Sing together.

Behold, behold, I make all things new,
beginning with you and starting from today.
Behold, behold, I make all things new,
my promise is true, for I am Christ the way.

"Behold, I Make All Things New"
John L. Bell, © 1994, The Iona Community,
GIA Publications, Inc., agent

Review and Apply

A **Work with Words**   Circle the letter of the correct answer.

1. Deliberate and serious acts by which you turn away from God are called _____.
   a. mortal sins   **b.** crimes   **c.** venial sins

2. Sins that weaken but do not destroy your relationship with God are called _____.
   a. mortal sins   **b.** crimes   **c.** venial sins

3. The gift from God that helps you know the difference between right and wrong is _____.
   a. natural law   **b.** conscience   **c.** sacrament

4. In the Sacrament of Reconciliation, a priest keeps secret whatever you confess because of the _____.
   a. covenant   **b.** sacramental seal   **c.** conscience

5. Jesus preached this parable about forgiveness: the parable of the _____.
   a. good shepherd   **b.** mustard seed   **c.** unforgiving servant

B **Make Connections**   What is your conscience?

_____

_____

_____

Activity Live Your Faith

Respond to an E-mail   A friend who is not Catholic e-mails you, asking why you confess your sins to a priest. Write your answer to your friend's question. Do your best to explain the benefits of the sacrament to your friend.

Mail

167

Family Faith

Catholics Believe

- Your conscience helps you know when you have sinned.
- Through the Sacrament of Reconciliation, God forgives sins and restores us to his friendship.

✝ SCRIPTURE

Read *Psalm 130* to find a message about forgiveness, kindness, and mercy.

GO ONLINE **www.harcourtreligion.com**
For weekly Scripture readings and seasonal resources

Activity

Live Your Faith

Give Examples of Forgiveness All people, at some time in their lives, have to ask forgiveness of others. Have each family member give an example of asking for forgiveness (no need to mention the offense) and explain what happened after that. Create a motto or choose a saying of Jesus that you can agree to live by as a forgiving family.

+ FORGIVE + AND + FORGET

People of Faith

Faustina was born in Poland. She was the third of ten children. When she was twenty, she entered the Congregation of Sisters of Our Lady of Mercy. In the 1930s, Faustina heard God's call to be an ambassador of mercy to the world through her writings and by bringing peace and joy to others. In 1938, on the verge of World War II, she died of tuberculosis at age thirty-three. She left behind a diary that recorded her mystical experiences. Faustina was canonized in 2000.

▲ Saint Faustina
Kowalska
1905–1938

Family Prayer

Saint Faustina, pray for us that we may trust in Jesus' mercy and work toward bringing about a forgiving world. Help us have a forgiving spirit toward others. Amen.

In Unit 5 your child is learning about MORALITY.

UNIT 5 REVIEW

A **Work with Words**   Use the clues provided to solve the puzzle.

Across

4. unjust structures in society

5. destroys relationship with God

7. inner voice giving advice

9. inner worth of a person

10. a state of tranquillity that is a
sign of God's kingdom

Down

1. Jesus' teachings about those who are blest

2. weakens relationship with God

3. giving God and others what is due to them

6. written in your heart

8. gift of the Holy Spirit prompting you to love

Unit 6
Sacraments

In this unit you will...

learn that the mission of the Church is to proclaim the gospel in word and deed. The Sacraments of Initiation give Christians new life and the strength to accomplish their mission of serving others. The Sacraments at the Service of Communion— Holy Orders and Matrimony — help bishops, priests, deacons and married couples live out their mission by following their vocation of service to others.

Chapter 16

Chapter 17

Chapter 18

What do you think you will learn in this unit about the Christian vocation?

Chapter 16 Baptized for Mission

 **Let Us Pray**

Leader: With the Spirit's help, we will continue your work, O Lord.

"So shall your rule be known upon the earth,
your saving power among all the nations."

Psalm 67:3

All: With the Spirit's help, we will continue your work, O Lord. Amen.

Activity  Let's Begin

On a Mission The word *mission* comes from a Latin word meaning "to send" and includes the idea of being sent to accomplish specific tasks. Some missions are simple. For example, you may be given the task of cleaning your room, or your teacher may send you to find paper supplies for your group.

At other times, your mission may be more serious. You might be sent to a neighbor's house to help watch young children or be asked to deliver an important message to a parent or teacher.

- Describe a mission that you were given that you took very seriously.

The Apostles' Mission

Focus How did the Apostles carry out Jesus' mission?

Jesus told his Apostles to continue his mission. He kept the promise he had made and sent the Holy Spirit to them at Pentecost. Then they were ready to carry out Jesus' mission. One day, God sent an angel with a message to Philip. This is Philip's story.

Philip and the Ethiopian

The angel instructed me to set out walking from Jerusalem on a desert road. Soon I spotted a chariot in front of me, and I heard the Spirit telling me to catch up with this chariot.

In the chariot, I saw a man from Ethiopia who was reading from the scroll of the prophet Isaiah.

"Do you understand what you are reading?" I asked the man.

"How can I, unless someone instructs me?" the man answered, gesturing to me to climb into the chariot. When I sat down with the man, I saw that he was reading a passage about the Servant of the Lord. I explained that the Servant of the Lord was Jesus. I told the man the good news of Jesus.

When we came to a pool of water, the man cried out, "Look, there is water. What is to prevent my being baptized?" So I baptized him in the pool. As soon as the man came out of the water, the Spirit led me away. The Ethiopian, meanwhile, continued on his way, rejoicing and praising God.

Based on Acts 8:26–39

❓ **Imagine that you have been asked to explain the good news of Jesus. What would you say?**

Your Mission

The story of Philip and the Ethiopian offers an example that you can follow as you continue the mission of Jesus. Like Philip, you are called to take any opportunity that comes your way to share the good news of Jesus. Through Philip, the Ethiopian experienced conversion of heart. After Philip baptized him, he began his own mission, going out "rejoicing and praising God."

Jesus has given you the Holy Spirit to help you on your **mission**. You, too, are empowered by the sacraments for your Christian mission. Through the liturgy and sacraments of the Church, you experience Jesus' presence and God's grace. You can rely on the Holy Spirit to accompany you on your mission. The kingdom of God is already present, but you will experience the fullness of God's kingdom at the end of time.

Words of Faith

For a Christian, **mission** is to be sent forth to share the good news of Jesus and God's kingdom.

Sacraments of Initiation

All Christians put on Christ and become members of his Church through the Sacrament of Baptism. In the early centuries of the Church, Baptism, Confirmation, and Eucharist were celebrated together. The person was baptized and sealed with the Spirit, and then joined the assembly at Eucharist for the first time. These three sacraments are called the Sacraments of Initiation because they mark the entry into the Christian life. Celebrating Baptism, Confirmation, and Eucharist together has again become the norm for adults and for some children entering the Church today.

Activity — Share Your Faith

Reflect: Think about a time when someone shared good news with you.

Share: With a partner, list three ways that you can share good news with others through words and actions.

_____

_____

_____

Act: Create a time line that represents the path of your life as a Christian, beginning with Baptism. Indicate when and how you can share good news in the future.

173

Sacraments of Initiation

How do you carry out the mission of Jesus today?

Baptism

The people of Jesus' time heard many stories involving water and new life. At creation, the Spirit moved over the waters. With Noah and the great flood, water brought about a new beginning. When Moses and the Israelites crossed the Red Sea, their passage through water was a sign of their delivery from slavery.

In the Gospel according to Mark, Jesus began his ministry by being baptized by John with water. This was not the sacrament as you know it today, although it had some of the same elements. Then, as now, it was a sign of conversion. Jesus submitted to John's baptism to show the people the importance of conversion.

Baptism also marks the beginning of your mission as a disciple of Jesus. This sacrament gives you a permanent and unrepeatable seal that marks you for Christ. You are sent by your Baptism to **evangelize**, or proclaim and share the good news. You are called to give witness to your faith through your words and actions.

A Royal Priesthood

Through Baptism, all the faithful share in the priesthood of Christ and in his prophetic and royal mission. This participation is called the priesthood of the baptized, or the priesthood of the faithful. This priesthood is different from the Sacrament of Holy Orders. This priesthood of the baptized is shared by every baptized Christian and exercised through a life filled with faith, hope, and charity.

 Why is Baptism the beginning of your Christian mission?

Confirmation

Confirmation perfects the grace of Baptism. This means that you are given the strength to carry out your mission of sharing the good news in word and action. Confirmation does this by a special outpouring of the gifts of the Holy Spirit, which seals or confirms you in Christ and unites you more closely with Jesus and the Church.

In Confirmation, a bishop, or sometimes a priest, anoints your forehead with **chrism**. This anointing is combined with the laying on of the bishop's or priest's hand and the words, "Be sealed with the Gift of the Holy Spirit." Confirmation, like Baptism, gives you a permanent spiritual mark. For this reason, you celebrate each of these sacraments only once in your life.

Eucharist

The Sacraments of Initiation conclude with the celebration of the Sacrament of Eucharist. At the altar you are united with the entire people of God. You offer yourself to God and participate in the sacrifice of Jesus. Responding to Jesus' assurance that his Body and Blood give life, you receive him in the consecrated Bread and Wine. You are nourished with the Bread of Life for your mission to go out and serve others. The Eucharist foretells eternal life in heaven.

❓ **Why do you think the celebration of the Eucharist completes the three Sacraments of Initiation?**

Words of Faith

To **evangelize** is to give witness to the faith by proclaiming the good news of Jesus Christ to the world through words and actions.

Chrism is blessed oil used for anointing in the Sacraments of Baptism, Confirmation, and Holy Orders.

Activity

Connect Your Faith

✏️ **Make a Crossword Puzzle** On a separate sheet of paper, make a crossword puzzle that includes the following words from the text: Baptism, chrism, Confirmation, Eucharist, evangelize, Initiation, mission, sacrament, priesthood, Spirit, bread, and water. Write a clue for each word.

Celebration of the Word

Let Us Pray

Gather and begin with the Sign of the Cross.

Sing together.

With the Spirit's gifts empower us
For the work of ministry.

"Lord, You Give the Great Commission", Jeffery Rowthon, © 1978, Hope Publishing Co.

Leader: With Baptism and Confirmation, Jesus sends us on a mission of evangelization. Listen as Jesus sends his disciples on such a mission.

Reader 1: A reading from the holy Gospel according to Luke.

Read Luke 9:1–6.

The Gospel of the Lord.

All: **Praise to you, Lord Jesus Christ.**

Reader 2: The spirit of the Lord God is upon me,
   because the Lord has anointed me;
He has sent me to bring glad tidings to the lowly,
   to heal the brokenhearted,
To proclaim liberty to the captives
   and release to the prisoners.

Reader 3: To announce a year of favor from the Lord
   and a day of vindication by our God,
   to comfort all who mourn.

Isaiah 61:1–2

Leader: Let us pray.

Bow your heads as the leader prays.

All: **Amen.**

A **Work with Words**   Match each description in Column 1 with the correct term in Column 2.

Column 1

_____ **1.** the foundational sacraments of Christian living

_____ **2.** common to all baptized people

_____ **3.** sacrament that begins the mission of a disciple

_____ **4.** blessed oil used for anointing

_____ **5.** proclaiming the good news of Jesus

Column 2

a. chrism

b. evangelization

c. Baptism

d. Sacraments of Initiation

e. priesthood of the baptized

B **Check Understanding**   Explain what happens in the Sacrament of Confirmation.

_____

_____

_____

Activity   Live Your Faith

Describe Your Christian Work   The call you receive at Baptism becomes a lifelong responsibility. Write a job description that explains for others your work as a Christian.

_____

_____

_____

_____

_____

_____

_____

_____

Family Faith

Catholics Believe

- The mission of the Church is to proclaim the Gospel in word and deed.
- Through the Sacraments of Initiation, Christians are given new life and are called to spread the good news.

✝ SCRIPTURE

Read *Acts 9:1–19* to learn about the conversion and Baptism of the greatest Christian missionary.

GO ONLINE www.harcourtreligion.com
For weekly Scripture readings and seasonal resources

Activity
Live Your Faith

Demonstrate Encouragement Contact your pastor or director of religious education to find out the names of those in your parish who are preparing for the Sacraments of Initiation. Choose a way to encourage one of these people, called catechumens, on his or her faith journey. You might invite the person over for dinner, send a card, or simply stop him or her before Mass on Sunday and offer a word of friendship and support.

People of Faith

Rose Duchesne lived her baptismal call as a religious sister. Born in France, she cared for those who were sick, educated children who were neglected, and sheltered priests during the French Revolution. In 1818 she left France for the United States. At St. Charles, Missouri, she established the first convent of the Religious of the Sacred Heart in the Americas. She opened a school in New Orleans, Louisiana. Among the Potawatomi tribe at Sugar Creek, Kansas, she shared the good news. They called her "woman who prays always." Saint Rose Philippine's feast day is November 18.

▲ **Saint Rose Philippine Duchesne 1769–1852**

Family Prayer

Saint Rose, pray for us that we may be courageous in living out our mission to share the good news of Jesus with others. We pray that we may be faithful to God's call. Amen.

In Unit 6 your child is learning about SACRAMENTS.

The Call to Ministry

Let Us Pray

Leader: Loving God, help us be your true servants.

"Gladden the soul of your servant;
to you, Lord, I lift up my soul."

Psalm 86:4

All: Loving God, help us be your true servants. Amen.

Activity — Let's Begin

What Is Service? Mr. Waters began the religion class with a question. "What is service?" he asked.

"I saw a picture of a silver tea service," said Latasha.

"My dad says you should tip for good service," offered Miguel.

"My parents attended a funeral service," Madison added.

"Let me ask the question a different way," said Mr. Waters. "What does it mean to serve?"

"My sister served food at a soup kitchen," said Shar.

"I am a server at Mass," Tyler said.

Mr. Waters asked another question: "How can you serve?"

• How would you answer Mr. Waters' last question?

Called to Serve

 **Focus** What is the meaning of the word *vocation*?

At the Last Supper, Jesus knew that the hour of his death was near. Knowing that he would not have another chance to teach his disciples before he went to the cross, Jesus did a surprising thing.

✝ **SCRIPTURE** The Gospel of John

The Washing of the Disciples' Feet

Faith Fact

Every year on Holy Thursday the Church follows the example of the washing of the feet as the priest washes the feet of members of the congregation.

Jesus got up from the table and poured water into a basin. He then knelt to wash his disciples' feet.

His disciples were very surprised at first. When it was Peter's turn, he objected by saying, "You will never wash my feet."

Jesus told him, "Unless I wash you, you will have no inheritance with me."

At this remark Peter looked serious and replied, "Master, then not only my feet, but my hands and head as well."

Then Jesus returned to his seat at the table. He asked his disciples, "Do you realize what I have done for you?" Then he explained, "If I, therefore, the master and teacher, have washed your feet, you ought to wash one another's feet."

Based on *John 13:1–15*

❓ **What did Jesus want his disciples to understand when he washed their feet?**

The Cost of Serving Others

In Jesus' time, people who were poor walked barefoot, and those of a higher class wore sandals. Washing the feet of guests when they entered a home was a job for servants—the owner of the house would not do it. It was shocking for Jesus' disciples to see him do such a thing.

Jesus' action was a sign that his disciples needed to be purified before they could enter his kingdom—just as you were purified by your Baptism. The washing of the disciples' feet was also a reminder that serving others would not always be easy. The disciples would have to humble themselves just as Jesus was about to be humbled by his passion and death. Serving others is always about thinking of what the other person needs and helping him or her, even when it is inconvenient or difficult to do so.

Your Vocation

Today, followers of Jesus usually are not asked to wash people's feet, but all Christians have the **vocation**, or call, to love and serve God and their neighbor.

When you are older, you may decide to live out your vocation by answering God's call to the ordained priesthood, to religious life, to marriage, or, perhaps, to the committed single life.

You may not yet know the vocation to which God is calling you. By praying, learning more about Jesus, and looking at the gifts and talents God has given you, you will discover your vocation.

Words of Faith

A **vocation** is a call to love and serve God and others.

Activity — Share Your Faith

Reflect: Make a list of what you are good at in school, at play, and at home.

Share: After you have shared your list, ask a classmate to suggest a kind of work that seems to suit you.

Act: Choose a life's work that would interest you, and write it on the top sandal. On the bottom sandal, write three ways that you could serve others in this vocation.

Holy Orders

 **Focus** How do priests and deacons live out their baptismal call?

Everyone who is baptized is called to continue the mission of Jesus by serving others. But some are called to ministry. **Ministry** is the special service that may include preaching the word and celebrating the sacraments. This work is given to men in ordained ministry through the Sacrament of Holy Orders.

Holy Orders confers a sacred power, through the laying on of hands by the bishop, for serving the faithful by teaching, leading the people in worship, and pastoral governing. Bishops, priests, and deacons all share in this Sacrament of Holy Orders, which is a sign of God's kingdom. Ordained men are marked forever as Christ's representatives.

? **Whom do you know in ordained ministry who has served you by helping you know more about Jesus?**

Bishop	Priest	Deacon
A bishop serves the Church as the pastor and teacher of his diocese. Bishops work with their fellow bishops and with the pope for the good of the whole Church.	Priests assist the bishop within a diocese. As pastor of a parish, a priest shares the bishop's work in the diocese. Priests celebrate the sacraments with the community.	Permanent deacons are ordained ministers who serve the diocese and parish by assisting in liturgical roles and by doing works of charity. Married men can be called to the order of permanent deacon.

Consecrated Life

Some priests live in religious communities in what is called **consecrated life**. Members of these communities dedicate themselves to serving God by following the charism, or special grace, of the community and its founder. There are also many communities of religious sisters. Members of religious communities may teach, care for the sick, work as missionaries, or do other good works.

Members of religious communities choose to live three **vows**, or sacred promises, that are found at the heart of the gospel—poverty, chastity, and obedience. Poverty is the choice to live a simple life and to share material possessions in community. Chastity is the choice to maintain the right balance of body and spirit in human sexuality. Chastity is also a virtue that requires the proper integration of sexuality according to one's state of life. For men and women religious, this means living a celibate life. Obedience is the choice to follow God's will as it is expressed through the guidance of the community's leaders, the charism of the community, and the individual's conscience.

Lives of Service

Those who accept the call to ordained priesthood or religious life choose lives of service for the sake of God's people. Because they are human, they can make mistakes. But they are always worthy of respect, because of their human dignity and their willingness to make a difficult and lifelong commitment in service to God's people.

Words of Faith

Ministry is the work of service by ordained ministers and, in certain circumstances, by laypeople.

The **consecrated life** is a state of life lived in community and characterized by the vows of poverty, chastity, and obedience.

Vows are promises made to God. Religious vows include the public profession of what are called the evangelical counsels: poverty, chastity, and obedience.

Activity — Connect Your Faith

Imagine Future Ministry   Imagine that it is twenty years from now and that God has called you to the ordained ministry or to the religious life.

What ministry can you imagine yourself doing?

_____

What gift would you bring to your ministry?

_____

What sacrifices would your ministry demand of you?

_____

183

Prayer of Petition

Let Us Pray

Gather and begin with the Sign of the Cross.

Leader: God our Father, bless all who serve you and others.

Reader 1: A reading from the Letter to the Hebrews.

Read Hebrews 5:1–6.
The word of the Lord.

All: **Thanks be to God.**

Reader 2: We ask that your ministers may grow to a greater love of Jesus.

All: **Lord, hear our prayer.**

Reader 3: We ask that the Holy Spirit may strengthen their hearts and enlighten their minds.

All: **Lord, hear our prayer.**

Reader 4: We ask that through their efforts and ours, in the power of the Holy Spirit, your kingdom on earth will continue to grow.

All: **Lord, hear our prayer.**

Leader: Let us pray.

Bow your heads as the leader prays.

All: **Amen.**

Sing together.

May the Lord,
mighty God,
bless and keep
you forever,
grant you peace,
perfect peace,
courage in ev'ry
endeavor.

"May the Lord, Mighty God"
Unknown

A **Check Understanding** Circle True if a statement is true and circle False if a statement is false. Correct any false statements.

1. All baptized people share in the Sacrament of Holy Orders.

   True   False   _____

2. Each religious community has a charism, or special gift, of service.

   True   False   _____

3. You share in the common priesthood of the faithful through your Baptism.

   True   False   _____

4. At the Last Supper, Jesus taught the disciples how to serve through his example of preparing the meal.

   True   False   _____

5. Members of religious communities make the vows of poverty, chastity, and obedience.

   True   False   _____

B **Make Connections** What is the difference between mission and ministry?

_____

_____

Activity — Live Your Faith

Learn About a Community Choose a religious community about which you would like to learn more. Research the community during the next week by reading an article or a part of a book or by investigating the community's Web site. Present your findings to your group the next time you meet.

Family Faith

Catholics Believe

- All of the baptized are called to follow Christ by serving others.

- Ordained ministers serve God through preaching the word and through celebrating the sacraments.

SCRIPTURE

Read *Hebrews 4:14—5:10* to learn how to participate in Christ's priesthood. As high priest and mediator, Christ has made the Christian community a kingdom and all believers priests for God.

GO ONLINE www.harcourtreligion.com
For weekly Scripture readings and seasonal resources

Activity

Live Your Faith

Interview a Servant Is there a member of your family who has been called to ministry in the Church? Interview your relative to find out more about how he or she experienced God's call. If there is no one in your family in ministry, ask someone in your parish—a priest, deacon, woman religious, or catechist, for example—to tell you about his or her ministry. You might invite the person to share a meal at your home.

People of Faith

▲ Saint John Neumann 1811–1860

After attending a diocesan seminary for theological training, **John Neumann** came to the United States from the Czech Republic. Soon after his arrival he was ordained a priest and served European immigrants on the frontier. He joined the Redemptorist Order and established many schools. Later, John was named bishop of Philadelphia. He encouraged religious orders to settle in the area. He also built a number of new parishes and began building a cathedral. His feast day is January 5.

Family Prayer

Saint John, pray for us that we may respond to God as he calls us to serve him and other people. Pray that each of us may have a servant's heart. Amen.

Chapter 18 Together in Love

 **Let Us Pray**

Leader: O God, help us fulfill our vows.

"Then I will sing your name forever,
fulfill my vows day after day."

Psalm 61:9

All: O God, help us fulfill our vows. Amen.

Activity — Let's Begin

A Time to Talk

When a friend calls to me from the road
And slows his horse to a meaning walk,
I don't stand still and look around
On all the hills I haven't hoed,
And shout from where I am, 'What is it?'
No, not as there is a time to talk.
I thrust my hoe in the mellow ground,
Blade-end up and five feet tall,
And plod: I go up to the stone wall
For a friendly visit.

Robert Frost

• Why is it important to take time to talk
  with friends?

Together in Holiness

Focus How is marriage a sacrament?

Good marriages are based on friendship. In the New Testament, marriage is an image of Christ's relationship with the Church. Jesus used wedding images in some of his parables.

A STORY

WEDDING AT CANA

My name is Mary, and my son's name is Jesus. Many people were invited to attend a wedding in the town of Cana. Jesus came with me, as did some of his friends.

During the wedding party, I noticed that the wine was running out. I turned to Jesus and said, "They have no wine." Jesus replied, "How does this concern of yours affect me?"

Then I said to one of the waiters, "Do whatever he tells you."

Jesus then pointed to six large water jars, each one able to hold twenty to thirty gallons. He instructed the waiters to fill the jars to the brim with water. When they had done this, he said, "Draw some out now and take it to the headwaiter."

The headwaiter tasted the water that was now wine. He said to the groom, "Everyone serves good wine first, and then when people have drunk freely, an inferior one; but you have kept the good wine until now."

This was the first miracle that Jesus worked.

? Why do you think Jesus performed his first miracle at a wedding feast?

Matrimony

Jesus' presence at the marriage at Cana showed his appreciation for marriage. Jesus taught that marriage is from God and cannot be broken by human choices. He said, "What God has joined together, no human being must separate." (See *Mark 10:9*.)

Because of Jesus' teaching, the Church recognizes marriage as a sacrament and gives it the name **Matrimony**. Marriage is a lifelong partnership of service with two purposes. It helps people grow together in holiness and love, and it creates the proper place for welcoming children and educating them in the practice of the faith.

❓ **Why do you think marriage is so important?**

Sacrament of Service

Matrimony is called a Sacrament at the Service of Communion. Married people share a unique covenant and have special responsibilities. A husband and wife pledge to live their lives in loving friendship and service to each other and to the community. By their mutual love and fidelity, they build up the whole community of faith and become a sign of salvation to all who witness their selfless love.

Words of Faith

Matrimony is a Sacrament of Service in which a man and woman make a covenant of love with each other and with God.

Activity _ Share Your Faith

Reflect: Among the married couples you know, who are signs of service to you?

Share: In a small group, brainstorm the qualities of a strong marriage.

Act: Choose what you consider the three most important qualities of a strong marriage, and write them in the links of the chain.

A Domestic Church

◎ Focus   How is the family a domestic Church?

One of Pope John Paul II's visits to the United States took place in 1987. During that visit he spoke about the importance of families. He said that the life of the parish greatly depends on the commitment and involvement of its families. The family is the basic unit of society and of the Church. The pope, however, was very realistic when he said that some families are healthy and filled with the love of God, some families have little energy for the Spirit, and some families have broken down altogether.

The Church has a concern for all families, and it ministers to them in the name of Jesus. Families are so important that they are called domestic Churches. A **domestic Church** is a church of the home, a family community of faith, hope, and charity. New members of the Church emerge from the family and, in the family, faith in Jesus is first nourished by word and example. In his 1991 letter on the family, Pope John Paul II said, "The family, called together by word and sacrament as the Church of the home, is both teacher and mother, the same as the worldwide Church."

❓ **In what way is your family a domestic Church? How could it be stronger?**

Sharing God's Love

The families that come from the union of marriage are meant to be living signs of faith for the Church and the world. With God's grace, husbands and wives follow Christ together in love, just as others may be called to do in Holy Orders, consecrated religious life, or a committed single life.

No matter what vocation of love and service to God and others you follow, you are required to live the virtues related to sexuality and to honor the ninth commandment.

Words of Faith

The family is called a **domestic Church** because it is the place where children first learn about God through the love, teaching, and good example of parents and other family members.

Purity of heart	is achieved with God's grace through temperance, chastity, modesty, and prayer.
Temperance	is the virtue that helps you use moderation in your actions, thoughts, and feelings.
Chastity	is the virtue that helps you remain pure in conduct and intention. In religious life or Holy Orders, chastity includes being celibate.
Modesty	is the virtue that leads you to dress, move, and talk in appropriate ways.

The practice of these virtues and sincere prayer bring you strength and lead you closer to God.

Welcome to Our Parish

Activity Connect Your Faith

Write a Letter On a separate sheet of paper, compose a letter to a couple, a single person, or a religious who is a sign of God's love to others. Describe the good example that he or she shows. Send the letter to the person.

Prayer of Blessing

Let Us Pray

Gather and begin with the Sign of the Cross.

Leader: God our Father, we ask your blessing on all married couples.

Reader 1: May the peace of Christ live always in the hearts and homes of all married couples.

Reader 2: May they be ready and willing to comfort all who come to them in need, and may they enjoy the blessings promised to the compassionate.

Reader 3: May their children bring them happiness, and may their generous love for their children be returned to them over and over again.

Reader 4: May they find happiness and satisfaction in their work.

Reader 5: May the Lord bless them with many happy years together so that they may enjoy the rewards of a good life.

Leader: Let us pray.

Bow your heads as the leader prays.

All: **Amen.**

Sing together.

For your gracious blessing,
for your wondrous word,
for your loving kindness,
we give thanks, O God.

"For Your Gracious Blessing"
Traditional

Review and Apply

A **Check Understanding** Circle the letter of the correct answer.

1. Jesus' first miracle in the Gospel according to John was _____.

   a. the multiplication of loaves   **b.** turning water into wine
   c. walking on water

2. The name the Church gives to the sacrament that celebrates God's blessing of married couples is _____.

   a. Matrimony   **b.** Eucharist   **c.** Holy Orders

3. Two purposes of marriage are to help people grow together in holiness and love and to create a place for welcoming _____.

   a. strangers   **b.** pets   **c.** children

4. He said: "The family, called together by word and sacrament as the Church of the home, is both teacher and mother, the same as the worldwide Church."

   a. Saint Peter   **b.** Jesus   **c.** Pope John Paul II

5. The basic unit of society and the Church is the _____.

   a. marriage   **b.** family   **c.** single life

B **Make Connections** Why is the family called a domestic Church?

_____

Activity Live Your Faith

Create a Song or Poem A good marriage is rooted in a deep friendship between husband and wife. Create a song or poem about such a marriage. Tell what it takes to make and maintain a good marriage.

_____
_____
_____
_____
_____
_____

Family Faith

Catholics Believe

- Matrimony helps a man and woman grow in love and holiness and prepare a home for children.

- The Church celebrates marriage through the Sacrament of Matrimony.

✝ SCRIPTURE

Read *Ephesians 5:21–33* to hear what Paul taught about how husbands and wives should treat each other.

GO ONLINE www.harcourtreligion.com
For weekly Scripture readings and seasonal resources

Activity

Live Your Faith

Strengthen Your Family No family matches exactly the ideal described in the New Testament. But God loves all families, and all families can grow stronger. One way to strengthen your family is to imagine yourselves as the best you can be. Make a collage that illustrates the ideals of the Sacrament of Matrimony. Put it in a prominent place as a reminder of the ideals of marriage and family life.

People of Faith

▲ **Saint Birgitta of Sweden 1304–1373**

Birgitta was from a noble family, the daughter of a governor. She became a major religious figure of the late Middle Ages. She was married for twenty-eight years and had eight children. After her husband died, Birgitta founded a religious community of men and women who lived in a double monastery with the abbess as superior. Birgitta worked and prayed tirelessly for justice and peace. Her *Revelations* record her life, including her visions and spiritual experiences. Saint Katherine of Sweden was her daughter. Saint Birgitta's feast day is July 23.

🌱 Family Prayer

Saint Birgitta, pray for us that we may help our families love Jesus and may be a source of peace and justice in our community. May we show purity, temperance, and chastity in our lives. Amen.

In Unit 6 your child is learning about SACRAMENTS.

UNIT 6 REVIEW

 Work with Words Complete each sentence with the correct term from the Word Bank.

WORD BANK

Baptism
vocation
Reconciliation
mission
sacrament
ministry
Matrimony
domestic
evangelize
consecrated
chrism
vows

1. A call to love and serve God is a _____.

2. A sending forth to share the good news of Jesus and God's kingdom is known as a _____.

3. _____ is a Sacrament of Service in which a man and woman make a covenant of love with each other and with God.

4. _____ is blessed oil used for anointing in the Sacraments of Baptism, Confirmation, and Holy Orders.

5. To _____ is to give witness to the faith by proclaiming the good news of Jesus Christ to the world through words and actions.

6. Families are the order God created and are so important that they are called _____ Churches.

7. _____ is the special service that may include preaching the word and celebrating the sacraments.

8. Some priests live in religious communities in what is called _____ life.

9. _____ are sacred promises made to God.

10. Christians become members of Christ's Church through the Sacrament of _____.

195

Unit 7
Kingdom of God

In this unit you will...

learn that when we celebrate the Eucharist we are connected through the communion of saints to the living Christian faithful and those who have died in Christ. The Church is called to work for the unity of all Christians and to reunite the Body of Christ. We know that God will triumph over evil when Christ comes again in glory.

Chapter **19**

Chapter **20**

Chapter **21**

What do you think you will learn in this unit about the journey to the kingdom?

Chapter 19 All the Faithful

Let Us Pray

Leader: Help us be faithful in our friendships, O Lord.

"The heavens praise your marvels, Lord,
  your loyalty in the assembly of the holy ones."

Psalm 89:6

All: Help us be faithful in our friendships, O Lord. Amen.

Activity — Let's Begin

What Is Friendship?

A real friend is one who walks in when the rest of the world walks out.

Mencius

Friends are those rare people who ask how we are and then wait to hear the answer.

Ed Cunningham

My best friend is the one who brings out the best in me.

Henry Ford

No person is your friend who demands your silence, or denies your right to grow.

Alice Walker

One of the best things in life is having friends and being with them. Knowing that you have a friend can make the world less lonely. Knowing how to be a friend can make life better for you and for other people.

• What qualities do you look for in a friend?

• What definition of friendship would you add to the ones shown here?

The Church Grows

◎ Focus What is the communion of saints?

The members of the first Christian community were joined to one another by bonds of faith, hope, and charity. They knew this was the way to live as Jesus did. Things were generously shared and distributed according to need. Here is Barnabas's description of his life in the early Christian community.

✝ SCRIPTURE — Acts of the Apostles

The Christian Community

I sold a piece of property that I owned. Then I brought the money I made from the sale and placed it at the feet of the Apostles in Jerusalem. I was called Joseph at the time, but the Apostles gave me a new name, Barnabas, which means "son of encouragement."

My gift of money was the least I could do to help the new community of Christians. All of us were of one heart and mind; what we owned was for the common good.

We devoted ourselves to the community and to following the teachings of the Apostles. Every day we met in the Temple area for prayer, and we met in our homes for the breaking of bread. We did this with great joy, praising God and enjoying the good will of the people.

Based on *Acts 2:42–47, 4:32–37*

❓ From the description in this passage, what does the phrase *common good* mean?

Communion of Saints

The first community of Christians was very small, but the Church today has grown to include many members all over the world. You are still connected today to Barnabas and the other early Christians.

The Church itself is often referred to as a **communion of saints**. This expression has two meanings. It refers first to the holy things, above all the Eucharist, by which the unity of the faithful is represented and brought about. The term also refers to the communion among all the faithful who are living today and those who have died and are in heaven or **purgatory**. The communion of saints is bound together by the love of the Holy Trinity.

Catholics believe that those who die in God's friendship but who are not completely converted are purified in purgatory before enjoying heaven. As a member of the communion of saints, you are encouraged by the Church to pray for the souls in purgatory.

Two very special days celebrated in the Church year are All Saints' Day on November 1 and All Souls' Day on November 2. All Saints' Day is a holy day of obligation. It honors all who live now with God in heaven. On All Souls' Day the Church prays for those who have died in friendship with God but are undergoing final purification before enjoying eternal happiness with him.

❓ **What deceased members of your family can you honor on All Saints' Day or All Souls' Day?**

Words of Faith

The **communion of saints**, when referring to holy persons, includes the pilgrim Church on earth, those being purified in purgatory, and the blessed already in heaven.

Purgatory is a state of final purification after death and before heaven.

Activity — Share Your Faith

Reflect: Review the stories of the people of faith about whom you have read in this book.

Share: With a partner, choose three of these people of faith and discuss the qualities that made them people of faith.

Act: Which of these qualities would you like to develop? Choose one quality, and tell how you will practice it this week.

_____

_____

_____

Charity and Prayer

Focus What do charity and prayer have to do with the communion of saints?

One virtue that links you directly with the communion of saints and the Trinity is charity. It is the virtue by which you love God above all things and by which you love others because you love God. It is one of the three virtues that relate directly to your relationship with God. Charity calls you to live as the Trinity lives, in perfect love.

In the scripture story about the first Christians, you saw an example of people practicing charity. Out of charity you use your resources—your time, your money, and your talents—to show your love of God by helping others in need. Charitable people provide for the physical needs of others through the Corporal Works of Mercy, such as feeding the hungry or visiting the sick. They also provide for the spiritual needs of others by performing the **Spiritual Works of Mercy**.

SPIRITUAL WORKS OF MERCY

- **Warn the sinner**—Caution those who are being led away from God and neighbor through sin.

- **Teach the ignorant**—Correct misunderstandings and prejudices based on ignorance and fear.

- **Counsel the doubtful**—Give spiritual advice to those who doubt their faith, themselves, or their relationships with others.

- **Comfort the sorrowful**—Show empathy to those who are lonely, grieving, and alienated.

- **Bear wrongs patiently**—Respond to the evil that is done to you in a way that doesn't cause more evil and suffering.

- **Forgive all injuries**—Forgive injuries so that they don't lead you toward bitterness and resentment.

- **Pray for the living and the dead**—Unite through prayer with the living and those in heaven and purgatory.

❓ Which Spiritual Work of Mercy do you already practice?

❓ Which one seems the hardest to do? Why?

Intercessory Prayer

In addition to performing works of mercy, you can pray for others. **Intercessory prayer** is interceding, or stepping between, God and others in the community of faith to ask God's help for them. You can pray for those who are close to you; for those around the world who suffer from hunger, poverty, disease, and war; and for those who have died and are not yet with God in heaven.

You can pray by using your own words to ask God's help for whatever you need. You can also use such traditional prayers as litanies. You can pray out loud or in silence, at Mass or in a peaceful place in nature. Others in the communion of saints will also intercede with God for you. You can ask Mary, the Mother of God, and all the saints to present your prayers before God.

❓ **What way to pray is easiest for you?**

Growing Stronger in Spirit

Every member of the communion of saints is important. As you grow stronger in your own relationship with God, you make the whole communion of saints stronger. One way to create stronger bonds is through your personal prayer.

One form of personal prayer is meditation. When you meditate, you use your mind, imagination, and emotions to listen to God and deepen your faith. For example, you can read a short passage from the Bible and ask the Holy Spirit to help you understand what God will say to you as you reflect on the scripture passage. Other thoughts and worries may enter your mind and distract you from prayer. Gently turn away from them and back to God.

Words of Faith

Spiritual Works of Mercy are actions that care for the spiritual needs of others.

Intercessory prayer is a form of prayer in which you pray to God on behalf of another.

Activity — Connect Your Faith

A Prayer Card Make a prayer card to remind yourself to pray for family members and friends, both living and dead, who are in need. On the card, write the names of the people you wish to remember in your prayers. Keep it with you every day.

Mom
Dad
Sheila
Aunt Kathy
Uncle Bill

Litany of the Saints

Let Us Pray

Gather and begin with the Sign of the Cross.

Leader: Holy Mary, Mother of God,

All: **Pray for us.**

Leader: Saint John the Baptist,

All: **Pray for us.**

Leader: Saint Mary Magdalene,

All: **Pray for us.**

Leader: Saint Ignatius,

All: **Pray for us.**

Leader: Saint Francis of Assisi,

All: **Pray for us.**

Leader: Saint Thérèse,

All: **Pray for us.**

Leader: All holy women and men,

All: **Pray for us.**

Leader: Lord, be merciful,

All: **Lord, save your people.**

Leader: By your death and rising to new life,

All: **Lord, save your people.**

By your gift of the Holy Spirit,

All: **Lord, save your people.**

All: **Amen.**

Sing together.

We sing of the saints filled with Spirit and grace,
Blest women and men through all time, from each place.
God chose them, the holy, the humble, the wise
To spread the Good News of salvation in Christ.

"We Sing of the Saints", Alan J. Hommerding, © 1994, World Library Publications, Inc.

CHAPTER 19

Review and Apply

A **Work with Words**   Complete the following statements.

1. Love of God and neighbor is called _____.

2. _____ is a form of prayer in which you use your mind, imagination, and emotions to listen to God and deepen your faith.

3. The state of final purification after death and before enjoying heaven is called _____.

4. Charitable people provide for the spiritual needs of others by performing _____.

5. When you ask God's help for others, you _____ for them.

B **Check Understanding**   Describe the communion of saints as it refers to holy persons.

_____

_____

_____

_____

_____

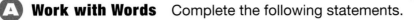

Activity Live Your Faith

Plan and Create a Poster   Create a poster with the title "What the World Needs Now." Fill your poster with images of people who are living the Spiritual Works of Mercy. Group the images according to the works that they show. Write the name of the appropriate Spiritual Work of Mercy under each group. Write your plan here.

_____

_____

_____

Family Faith

Catholics Believe

- Members of the communion of saints can intercede, or pray to God for others.

- The communion of saints includes all holy persons, both living and dead, who are united in the Eucharist.

✚ SCRIPTURE

Read *Romans 14:1–12* to learn about Paul's teaching on living and dying for Christ.

GO ONLINE **www.harcourtreligion.com**
For weekly Scripture readings and seasonal resources

Activity
Live Your Faith

Remember Your Loved Ones Help one another hold in memory your relatives and friends who have died. Create a special memory book with stories and other information about the lives of these people. Write a family prayer for them, and place it on the first page of the book. Pray this prayer together whenever you look through the book.

People of Faith

Elizabeth Ann Seton is the first saint who was born in the United States. She was married and the mother of five children. After her husband died, Elizabeth became a Catholic. She was deeply committed to helping people who were poor. In 1809, with four companions, she founded the Daughters of Charity of St. Joseph. She opened a school in Emmitsburg, Maryland, for children who were poor. Elizabeth is considered to be a founder of the parochial school system in the United States. Her feast day is January 4.

▲ Saint Elizabeth Ann Seton 1774–1821

🌷 Family Prayer

Saint Elizabeth Ann, pray for us that we may imitate your charity toward those in need. May we intercede daily for the needs of others. Amen.

Chapter 20 Christians as One

Let Us Pray

Leader: God of all people, unite us in your truth.

"You, LORD, are near to all who call upon you,
to all who call upon you in truth."

Psalm 145:18

All: God of all people, unite us in your truth. Amen.

Activity — Let's Begin

A Family Dinner It was time for Thanksgiving dinner. The food was ready, and the table was set. Everyone was there except Patrick's favorite relative, Aunt Katie. Patrick wondered: Was there some kind of family quarrel going on that made her decide not to attend? Or hadn't she been invited?

When he asked his mom about Aunt Katie, she just said, "Don't ask!" As he sat at the dinner table, Patrick silently wished that people could just get along with one another.

• What happens when divisions occur within families?

Unity and Division

◎ Focus What did Jesus teach about unity?

On the evening of the Last Supper, Jesus spoke to his disciples about the importance of unity.

The Prayer of Jesus

While Jesus was sitting with his friends around the table, He said to them, "Behold, the hour is coming and has arrived when each of you will be scattered to his own home and you will leave me alone. ... In the world you will have trouble, but take courage, I have conquered the world."

Then Jesus prayed, "Holy Father, keep them in your name that you have given me, so that they may be one just as we are. ... I pray not only for them, but also for those who will believe in me through their word, so that they may all be one, as you, Father, are in me and I in you, that they also may be in us, that the world may believe that you sent me."

Based on *John 16:32–33, 17:11, 20–21*

One of the most precious gifts of the Church is the unity that comes from Jesus. The Church has one Lord, one faith, and one Baptism. Jesus formed his followers into one Body and gave it the life of one Spirit.

❓ Why do you think unity was so important to Jesus?

The Story Continues

Before the Last Supper was over, Judas had left to arrange for Jesus' arrest. Like the history of the Israelites, the history of the Church is a story of heroes and holiness. But there are also times of sin and failure along the way.

As time went on, other people tested the unity of the Church. Because of this, Paul wrote to the Corinthians, urging them to be united in the same mind and purpose. (See *1 Corinthians 1:10–13.*)

Words of Faith

A **schism** is a break or division.

The **Protestant Reformation** was a sixteenth-century religious separation from the Catholic Church that began with Martin Luther's preaching against errors he saw in the Church.

More Divisions

Martin Luther, **by Russell Goodman**

In A.D. 1054, a **schism**, or division, occurred between the Church in the East and the Church in the West. Leaders quarreled about authority, Church practices, and Church teaching. The Great Schism, as it was called, continues to this day. The Eastern Orthodox Churches remain divided from the Catholic Church.

In the 1500s the Catholic Church experienced another division. A priest named Martin Luther spoke out against errors he saw in the Church. His action led to the **Protestant Reformation**. Luther and several other Christian leaders and groups separated from the authority of the pope. The unity of the Church in the West was shattered. Despite improvements, Protestants and Catholics are still separated today.

Activity — Share Your Faith

Reflect: Review the story of the Church's divisions.

Share: With a partner, create a visual summary of the story of the Church's divisions that are described on this page. Choose an image that will symbolize the divisions that occurred. Add captions along the way to identify key events.

Act: Write one way that you contribute to unity among the churches.

_____

_____

New Hope

⊚ **Focus**   What is ecumenism?

Today there are many different denominations of Protestant Christians. A denomination is a Christian religious group with its own organization, worship, and set of beliefs. Since the Protestant Reformation, denominations have continued to subdivide. These splits have occurred because people have disagreed about such issues as biblical interpretation, authority, and worship.

Division among Christians has been a sad reality for a long time. For many centuries various Christian groups spoke and acted like enemies. They ignored the love and unity in Jesus that was their bond as Christians.

In the early 1900s, representatives of many Christian groups gathered to talk about working in harmony. They admitted that division is not what Jesus wanted for his followers. Realizing that they had neglected working for unity in Jesus, they began the ecumenical movement. The word **ecumenism** comes from a Greek biblical phrase that means "the whole household of God." The purposes of this organized effort are to bring Christians together in a spirit of cooperation and to look forward in hope to the restoration of unity among Christians.

❓ **In what ways can you bring about a more united Church?**

Ecumenism Today

The ecumenical movement was one of the important issues Catholic bishops from around the world discussed during the Second Vatican Council. This Church council took place in Rome between 1962 and 1965. The bishops agreed that unity among Christians was Christ's desire for the Church and that the divisions between Christians should not be ignored.

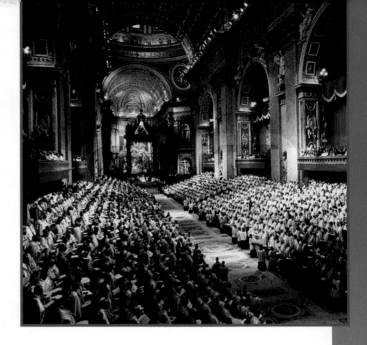

The bishops outlined steps that Christians could take to encourage the spirit of ecumenism. Unity would be possible only if Christians from different groups began to talk to one another. Christians should share their faith by joining together for prayer and acts of service. The various churches should focus on what unites them rather than on what divides them.

✝ SCRIPTURE

"As a body is one though it has many parts," wrote Paul, "and all the parts of the body, though many, are one body, so also Christ."

See 1 Corinthians 12:12.

You can work with other Christians to further the unity for which Jesus prayed. You can open doors to understanding by listening to and respecting the views of others while holding fast to your own. Place your hope for unity in the power of the Holy Spirit. Pray to the Spirit to make Christianity one, as Jesus and the Father are one.

Ecumenism is an organized effort to bring Christians together in cooperation as they look forward in hope to the restoration of the unity of the Christian Church.

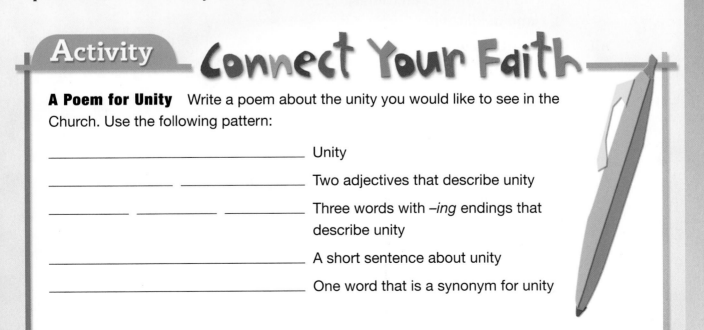

Activity — Connect Your Faith

A Poem for Unity   Write a poem about the unity you would like to see in the Church. Use the following pattern:

_____ Unity

_____ _____ Two adjectives that describe unity

_____ _____ _____ Three words with –ing endings that describe unity

_____ A short sentence about unity

_____ One word that is a synonym for unity

© Harcourt Religion

Prayer of Petition

Let Us Pray

Gather and begin with the Sign of the Cross.

Leader: The Lord be with you.

All: **And also with you.**

Leader: Lord, give us the strength to live in a manner worthy of the call we have received.

All: **Lord, show us how to be one.**

Leader: Give us the grace to act with all humility and gentleness, with patience, bearing with one another through love.

All: **Lord, show us how to be one.**

Leader: Guide us so that we move toward unity and peace.

All: **Lord, show us how to be one.**

Leader: We are one body and have one Spirit and are called together with one hope.

All: **Lord, show us how to be one.**

Leader: You have given us one Lord, one faith, one Baptism, one God and Father of all, who is over all things, through all things, and in all things.

All: **Lord, show us how to be one. Amen.**

Based on *Ephesians 4:1–6*

Sing together.

All are welcome, all are welcome, all are welcome in this place.

"All Are Welcome", Marty Haugen, © 1994, GIA Publications, Inc.

© Harcourt Religion

A **Work with Words**   Circle the letter of the correct answer.

1. Jesus' prayer that "all may be one, as you, Father, are in me and I in you," is a prayer for _____.
   a. unity   b. division   c. justice

2. The break that occurred between the Church in the East and the Church in the West is called the _____.
   a. Second Vatican Council   b. Protestant Reformation   c. Great Schism

3. In the 1500s Martin Luther spoke against the abuses in the Church. This gave rise to the _____.
   a. Great Schism   b. Second Vatican Council   c. Protestant Reformation

4. Since the Protestant Reformation, many independent Christian groups have formed; these are called _____.
   a. ecumenism   b. denominations   c. schisms

5. In the 1960s ecumenism was one of the issues discussed by bishops from around the world at the _____.
   a. Second Vatican Council   b. Council of Trent   c. First Vatican Council

B **Check Understanding**   Explain the meaning of *ecumenism,* and give an example.

_____

_____

Activity Live Your Faith

Share Common Beliefs   Choose a friend, relative, or classmate whose religious beliefs differ from yours. Ask the person to tell you some of the things that he or she believes. Then share some of your own beliefs. Make a diagram like the one shown here, comparing your beliefs.

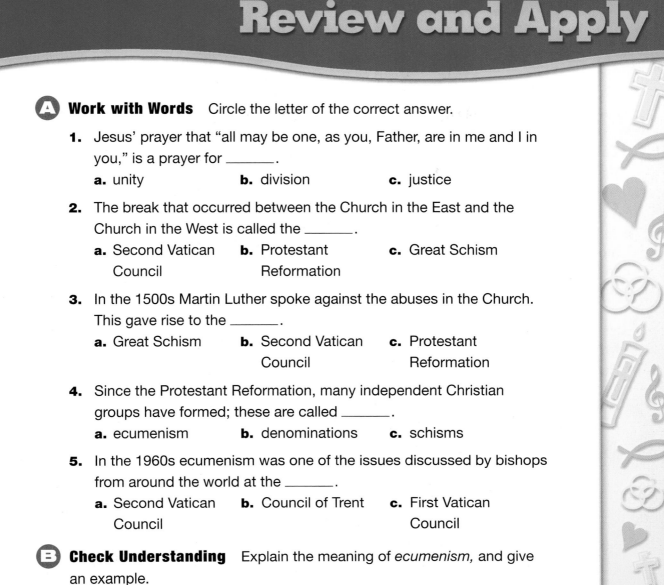

Family Faith

◎ Catholics Believe

■ Catholics work to reunite the Body of Christ because God desires the unity of Christians.

■ Today the ecumenical movement looks for ways to help all Christians work toward unity.

✝ SCRIPTURE

Read *1 Corinthians 12:12–26* to learn about an image of the Church as one body with many parts.

GO ONLINE **www.harcourtreligion.com**
For weekly Scripture readings and seasonal resources

Activity

Live Your Faith

Discuss Common Beliefs Some families of other Christian denominations probably live in your neighborhood. Decide on one thing your family can do that will show a spirit of ecumenism. For example, invite someone who is Protestant to dinner and discuss common beliefs.

• Before the person visits, do some research in the library or on the Internet about his or her denomination.

• Be prepared to say clearly and simply what your family believes.

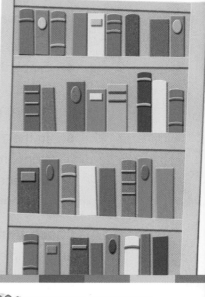

People of Faith

Charles was born into an aristocratic family in Italy. His uncle became Pope Pius IV. Charles, who became a priest, bishop, and cardinal, worked hard to correct the mistakes that had contributed to divisions within Christianity that resulted from the Protestant Reformation. Charles worked on the drafting of the catechism produced by the Council of Trent. Because of his efforts to reform the training of priests, Saint Charles Borromeo is the patron saint of seminarians. His feast day is November 4.

▲ **Saint Charles Borromeo 1538–1584**

🙌 Family Prayer

Saint Charles, pray for us that we may work toward the unity of all Christians. Help us accept those whose beliefs differ from our own. Amen.

Chapter 21 A New Creation

Let Us Pray

Leader: O God, help us put our hope in you.
"And now, Lord, what future do I have?
You are my only hope."

Psalm 39:8

All: O God, help us put our hope in you. Amen.

© Harcourt Religion

Activity — Let's Begin

Good Triumphs Picture a group of savage cave dwellers invading a group of peaceful cave dwellers. At first, chaos, bloodshed, and injustice prevail. But finally the peaceful cave dwellers fight back, expel the invaders, and live happily ever after.

Fast-forward to a spaceship in the future. Alien creatures gain entry to the ship. Murder and madness follow. Then the brave captain collects her forces and drives the creatures back into outer space.

Stories of the triumph over evil are as old as humanity itself.

• What stories have you read or watched that use the theme of good triumphing over evil?

The Triumph of Good

Focus What is the Book of Revelation about?

The ultimate victory of good over evil will take place when Christ comes in glory. You can read about the victory over evil in the Book of Revelation. Its author might have written a letter like this.

A LETTER

Dear Christians,

My name is John. Because of my faith in Jesus Christ, I have been exiled to the island of Patmos, a rocky island in the Aegean Sea. I wrote the Book of Revelation, and now I am writing to you to explain my book.

To understand the book, you must not take my images and symbols literally. The symbols are meant not only to describe the end of the world, but also to give hope and assurance to Christians.

I wrote the book as a form of **apocalyptic literature**. The word *apocalyptic* refers to something that is revealed, or unveiled. The Book of Revelation unveils the reality of God. I used symbols and numbers to unveil a message for my oppressed and persecuted sisters and brothers.

The message is simple: God will triumph over evil. He will give life to all who have died for their faith. Jesus will return and bring about a new world in which peace and justice last forever.

Your brother in Christ,
John

? **What is John's message for Christians today?**

Unveiling the Future

Toward the end of the first century, the Roman Emperors Nero and Domitian ordered that Christians be persecuted. Many followers of Jesus grew fearful as they watched their friends and family members sent to their deaths. These Christians wanted assurance that their faithfulness would be rewarded. They found that assurance in the Book of Revelation.

The writer of Revelation says that the revelation came to him in visions. Someone "like a son of man," with a face as bright as the sun, spoke to him. He meant Jesus. (See *Revelation 1:12–16.*) The writer was given seven messages for seven churches. The seven messages included visions that were meant for the whole Church everywhere.

After these messages, Revelation describes many more visions. In one, the writer sees the greatness and glory of God. He meets "the Lamb who was slain," another image of Jesus. The Lamb is handed a scroll closed with seven seals. Each opened seal sets loose a frightening image of death. The opening of the seventh seal begins a new cycle of seven angels blowing trumpets. Each trumpet blast sends a new plague upon the earth. The seventh trumpet, however, promises that God's new creation is coming soon. (See *Revelation 5:6—11:19.*)

Other visions follow, but this promise is repeatedly made: God will triumph over evil. The old world is ending. A new world is coming.

Words of Faith

Apocalyptic literature is a type of writing that claims to reveal what humans cannot see.

KEY TO REVELATION

Numbers
- **4** = the world
- **6** = imperfection
- **7** = perfection or completion
- **12** = Israel or the Apostles
- **666** = imperfection or evil
- **1,000** = a huge amount or a long time

Symbols
- **7 churches** = the entire Church everywhere
- **7 horns and eyes of the Lamb** = all power and all knowledge
- **24 elders** = the 12 tribes of Israel and the 12 Apostles
- **144,000 in white robes** = people of every nation; those invited into the new creation

Activity — Share Your Faith

Reflect: What evils do you hope God will triumph over today?

Share: In a small group, name the evils you have reflected on and pray for God's victory over them.

Act: Write a message to people your age about staying hopeful in the midst of the troubles of the world.

_____

_____

_____

Hope for the Future

◎ Focus What is God's new creation?

The Resurrection of Jesus is the source of Revelation's hope and optimism. By his Resurrection, Jesus triumphed over death and transformed death into life. He changed the curse of death into a blessing. Those who are put to death for their faith will be raised from the dead. Those who mourn their martyred friends and family members are reassured by the Book of Revelation that death is not the end.

Because Jesus has been raised from the dead, you will be raised, too. When you were baptized, you were raised from the death of sin to a new life with God the Father, the Son, and the Holy Spirit. After you die, having lived the promises of your Baptism, you will live with God forever.

Your body will someday die, just as Jesus' body died on the cross. But your body will be raised to new life, just as Jesus was raised from the dead. In the Old Testament, God gradually revealed the reality of bodily resurrection. So when Jesus was raised from the dead, his followers were able to accept the reality of a living, breathing, triumphant Jesus returned from the dead in a glorified body.

Faith Fact

Although the Old Testament contains very few references to life after death, it often mentions *sheol,* presented as a place of no movement, the destination of all souls after death.

City of Jerusalem, showing different buildings that are important to major religions

❓ How can your belief in the Resurrection affect the way you live today?

New Creation

The Book of Revelation's final vision is of a **new creation**. God promises that this new creation will include new heavens and a new earth ruled by God's justice. (See *2 Peter 3:13*.) Good will be rewarded and evil punished. The righteous, those who seek God sincerely and try to do his will, will reign with God forever. Even good people who have not been baptized will be with God.

The reign of God has already begun with Jesus. It is present in the Church, the beginning of the new Jerusalem, which is the beginning of the kingdom of God on earth.

The Bible begins with the story of creation in Genesis. It ends with the story of the new creation in Revelation. These stories tell you that the world began and will end according to God's design.

Words of Faith

The **new creation** is the future of justice, love, and peace promised by God, in which good will be rewarded and evil punished.

The Berlin Wall

Activity — Connect Your Faith

The "New Jerusalem"   Read *Revelation 21:1–4*. In a poem or drawing, tell or show what the "new Jerusalem" will look like.

Prayer of Petition

Let Us Pray

Gather and begin with the Sign of the Cross.

Leader: Lord, you said, "I am the Alpha and the Omega . . . the one who is and who was and who is to come, the almighty."

Revelation 1:8

Reader: The Lord be with you.

All: **And also with you.**

Reader: A reading from the holy Gospel according to John.

Read John 14:1–3.

The Gospel of the Lord.

All: **Praise to you, Lord Jesus Christ.**

Leader: Those whom the Lord has ransomed will return. They will come together with joy, and their sorrow will disappear.

All: **Come, Lord Jesus.**

Leader: The Lord will destroy death and wipe away tears from the faces of the faithful.

All: **Come, Lord Jesus.**

Leader: The Lord will create new heavens and a new earth. Everything in the past will be forgotten.

All: **Come, Lord Jesus.**

Leader: As a mother comforts her children, the Lord will comfort his daughters and sons.

All: **Come, Lord Jesus. Amen.**

Based on Isaiah 25:8, 35:10, 65:17, 66:13

Sing together.

Bring forth the Kingdom of mercy,
Bring forth the Kingdom of peace;
Bring forth the Kingdom of justice,
Bring forth the City of God!

"Bring Forth the Kingdom", Marty Haugen,
© 1986, GIA Publications, Inc.

Review and Apply

A **Work with Words**   Match each description in Column 1 with the correct term in Column 2.

Column 1

_____ **1.** These people sincerely seek God and want to do his will.

_____ **2.** This word means "revealed" or "unveiled."

_____ **3.** The central message of this book is that God will triumph over evil.

_____ **4.** This is the source of hope and optimism in the Book of Revelation.

_____ **5.** This is the final vision in the Book of Revelation.

Column 2

a. apocalyptic

b. Gospel of John

c. Resurrection

d. the righteous

e. the new creation

f. Revelation

B **Check Understanding**   Describe the new creation promised by God.

_____

_____

Activity   Live Your Faith

Draw a Symbol

Choose one or more of the symbols used in the Book of Revelation. Draw the symbol on a poster, and create a positive message for the world today that uses your symbol. Design your poster here.

Family Faith

⊙ Catholics Believe

■ God will triumph over evil when Christ comes again in glory.

■ In the new creation, God will reward good and punish evil.

✝ SCRIPTURE

Read *1 Corinthians 15:35–58* to learn from Paul why we should have hope for the future.

GO ONLINE www.harcourtreligion.com
For weekly Scripture readings and seasonal resources

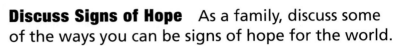

Activity

Live Your Faith

Discuss Signs of Hope As a family, discuss some of the ways you can be signs of hope for the world.

I can be a sign of hope by	This will help because

People of Faith

▲ Saint John the Evangelist c. 4–104

John, born in Galilee, was the son of Zebedee and Salome and the younger brother of James the Greater. He was a fisher until, with James, Jesus called him to be an Apostle. John is present in many Gospel accounts and was the only Apostle known to have been present at the crucifixion. At that time Jesus placed Mary in his care. John is traditionally associated with five books of the New Testament. He is often identified as the Beloved Disciple of the fourth Gospel, but this identification is uncertain. Saint John's feast day is December 27.

🙌 Family Prayer

Saint John, pray for us that we may follow in the footsteps of Jesus. May we have hope in the coming of Jesus and his kingdom. Amen.

In Unit 7 your child is learning about the KINGDOM OF GOD.

UNIT 7 REVIEW

A Work with Words   Circle the letter of the correct answer.

1. The communion of saints includes _____.

   a. the pilgrim Church on earth   b. those being purified in purgatory

   c. the blessed in heaven   d. all of these

2. The action that is *not* an example of a Spiritual Work of Mercy is _____.

   a. teaching the ignorant   b. feeding the hungry

   c. comforting the sorrowful   d. bearing wrongs patiently

3. A book of the Bible that is apocalyptic in nature is _____.

   a. Genesis   b. Psalms

   c. Revelation   d. Romans

4. Because Jesus has been raised, _____.

   a. death has been defeated   b. everyone will go to heaven

   c. no one will physically die again d. evil no longer exists

5. Ecumenism is an organized effort to _____.

   a. stop world hunger   b. end all wars

   c. bring all peoples together   d. bring Christians together

B Check Understanding   Match each description in Column 1 with the correct term in Column 2.

Column 1	Column 2
_____ 6. son of encouragement	a. Jesus
_____ 7. "I have conquered the world."	b. the Lamb
_____ 8. arranged for Jesus' arrest	c. John
_____ 9. wrote an apocalyptic book	d. Judas
_____ 10. opens a scroll with seven seals	e. Barnabas

CATHOLIC SOURCE BOOK

The Books of the Bible

The Catholic *canon,* or authorized version, of the Bible contains seventy-three books—forty-six in the Old Testament and twenty-seven in the New Testament.

The Old Testament
The Pentateuch

Genesis, Leviticus, Deuteronomy, Exodus, Numbers

The Historical Books

Joshua, 2 Samuel, 2 Chronicles, Judith, Judges, 1 Kings, Ezra, Esther, Ruth, 2 Kings, Nehemiah, 1 Maccabees, 1 Samuel, 1 Chronicles, Tobit, 2 Maccabees

The Wisdom Books

Job, Proverbs, Song of Songs, Psalms, Ecclesiastes, Wisdom, Sirach (Ecclesiasticus)

The Prophetic Books

Isaiah, Daniel, Jonah, Zephaniah, Jeremiah, Hosea, Micah, Haggai, Lamentations, Joel , Nahum, Zechariah, Baruch, Amos, Habakkuk, Malachi, Ezekiel, Obadiah

The New Testament
The Gospels

Matthew, Mark, Luke, John

The Acts of the Apostles
Epistles

Romans, 1 Corinthians, 2 Corinthians, Galatians, Ephesians, Philippians, Colossians, 1 Thessalonians, 2 Thessalonians, 1 Timothy, 2 Timothy, Titus, Philemon, Hebrews

The Catholic Epistles

James, 1 Peter, 2 Peter, 1 John, 2 John, 3 John, Jude

The Book of Revelation

The Book of Revelation is an example of apocalyptic literature. Apocalyptic means "revealed" or "unveiled." Apocalyptic writings reveal the secrets of heaven or the future by an angel or the Risen Christ. They were written to give hope to a suffering people. This form of writing began in Old Testament times and continued through the first century A.D.

The Book of Revelation uses numbers, colors, and other items as symbols. In this book, symbols hid messages from the Romans, who were persecuting Christians early in the Church's history.

Catholic Bibles

Catholic Bibles have seven Old Testament books or parts of books not included in other Christian Bibles. When these books are included in a Protestant Bible, they are usually found in a section called the *Apocrypha* or *Deutero-canonical Books*. The word *apocrypha* comes from a Greek word that means "hidden things."

The apocryphal books are not found in the present Hebrew Bible but were included in an early Jewish canon that included Greek writings. Protestant Reformers of later centuries did not accept these books. Catholic translations of the Bible include *The New American Bible* and *The New Jerusalem Bible*. Some translations, such as *The New Revised Standard Version*, are accepted by Catholics and Protestants.

Faith Fact

Wisdom

It is common for wisdom to be described as a person. In the Old Testament wisdom is a "she" in the form of a divine person. The name *Sophia* is the Greek word for wisdom. Christians see wisdom pictured in Jesus.

Rev. Peter Klein, *The Catholic Source Book*.

Salvation History

The history of salvation begins with creation, reaches its highest point in Christ, and lasts until the end of time. It is the story told in the Bible—the story of God's saving actions for humans. Important events of salvation history in the Old Testament include God's promise to Abraham, the Exodus, the covenant given to Moses, the Israelites' entering the land of Canaan, and the establishment of the kingdom of Israel under David. In the New Testament, salvation history is seen as coming together in the life, death, and Resurrection of Jesus. The Church continues to participate in salvation history.

Gospel Formation

The Gospels according to Matthew, Mark, Luke, and John announce the good news of Jesus to Christians today. These books were formed in three stages:

1. **The life and teaching of Jesus** Jesus' whole life and teaching proclaimed the good news.
2. **Oral tradition** After the Resurrection, the Apostles preached the good news. Then the early Christians passed on what Jesus preached. They told and retold the teachings of Jesus and the story of his life, death, and Resurrection.
3. **The written Gospels** The stories, teachings, and sayings of Jesus were collected and written in the Gospels according to Matthew, Mark, Luke (the synoptic, or similar Gospels), and John.

How to Better Understand Scripture

God is the author of Sacred Scripture. But he used human authors and inspired them to write the contents of the Bible. Catholics believe the Bible is a religious book and not an eyewitness account of historical events. For this reason, the words are not to be taken literally (word-for-word), but more for their spiritual sense or meaning. You need to take into account the context in which the human authors were writing. They were writing for a particular time and place and for a particular group of people. The writers were also using particular literary forms. You should always rely on the guidance of the Holy Spirit and the Church to help you interpret the religious truths of Scripture.

Storytelling in the Bible

The following are some of the types of literature found in the Bible.

Apocalypse writing reveals or unveils and usually uses very symbolic language. This form of writing is found in the Book of Daniel and the Book of Revelation.

Historical accounts were written to reveal God's activity in the world. The Book of Joshua is an example of a historical account.

Letters, or epistles, were addressed to early Christians by the Apostles and other early Church leaders.

Legends are stories from the past that are thought of as historical but have not been proven to be true.

Myths are traditional stories about historical events that help explain why people see things a certain way.

Oracles are messages from God spoken by prophets. They are often introduced by the words "Thus says the Lord."

Parables are short stories told by Jesus to make a point.

Psalms and canticles are poems and prayers that were once sung.

Sagas are long detailed accounts about people and events.

Titles of Jesus in Scripture

Jesus' followers used several different names for him. These names showed people's understanding of who Jesus was.

Christ means "the anointed one" in the Greek language.

Jesus is Jesus' common Jewish name; it means "God saves."

Lord is used to acknowledge Jesus' divinity.

Messiah is the Hebrew word for "the anointed one." The Messiah fulfills Jewish hope.

Rabbi means "teacher."

Faith Fact

Sarah, Miriam, Deborah, Hannah, Abigail, Hulda, and Esther are named as prophets in the Old Testament. Anna is the only prophetess named in the New Testament.

Rev. Peter Klein, *The Catholic Source Book.*

Mary in the Bible

- The angel visits Mary to announce her favor with God. *Luke 1:30*
- Mary visits Elizabeth to help her during her pregnancy. *Luke 1:39–40*
- Mary goes with Joseph to Bethlehem, where she gives birth to Jesus. *Luke 2:1–7*
- The magi visit Jesus with Mary. *Matthew 2:11*
- Mary, Joseph, and Jesus flee to Egypt and then return to Nazareth. *Matthew 2:13, 20*
- Mary and Joseph take the child Jesus to the Temple for presentation. *Luke 2:33–35*
- Mary and Joseph find the boy Jesus teaching in the Temple. *Luke 2:41–47*
- Mary is present at the wedding at Cana. *John 2:1–5*
- Mary comes to speak to Jesus when he is teaching his disciples. *Matthew 12:47–49, Mark 3:31–34, Luke 8:19–21*
- Mary is present at the foot of Jesus' cross. *John 19:25*
- Mary is in the upper room with the first community in Jerusalem. *Acts 1:14*

The Rosary and Scripture

Early Christians used beads or knotted strings to keep count of prayers. As devotion to Mary increased, it became popular to create psalters or books dedicated to Jesus or Mary, using biblical scenes. The Rosary we know today developed from both of these practices. As you pray each decade of beads, you think of one mystery in the life of Jesus or Mary.

The Mysteries of the Rosary

Joyful Mysteries	Sorrowful Mysteries	Glorious Mysteries	Luminous Mysteries
Annunciation	Agony in the Garden	Resurrection	The Baptism of Christ in the Jordan
Visitation	Scourging	Ascension	Jesus' Self-manifestation at the Wedding Feast of Cana
Nativity	Crowning with Thorns	Coming of Holy Spirit	The Announcement of the Kingdom Along with the Call to Conversion
Presentation	Carrying the Cross	Assumption	The Transfiguration
Finding Jesus in the Temple	Crucifixion	Coronation of Mary as Queen of Heaven	The Institution of the Eucharist as the Sacramental Expression of the Paschal Mystery
Heaven			

Creed

A creed is a summary of the Christian faith. The word *creed* means "I believe."

Marks of the Church

The Catholic Church is the Church founded by Christ and his Apostles. There are four marks, or characteristics of the Church. They are mentioned in the Nicene Creed.

- *One* means all the members are united as the Body of Christ, given life by the one Spirit. They acknowledge one Lord, one faith, one Baptism.
- *Holy* means the Church is centered in God. It is Christ who, by his sacrifice, makes the Church holy.
- *Catholic* means universal. The Church has the fullness of faith and is the means of salvation for all. The Church is for all times and all people.
- *Apostolic* means the Church is built on the foundation of the Apostles. It teaches the doctrine of Jesus as it has been handed down through the Apostles and their successors, the pope and bishops.

Mission

The Church's mission is to proclaim and further God's reign in the world. The Church continues the mission, or work, of Christ through the Holy Spirit, according to God's plan. This work is done by all Christians—clergy, laity, and religious.

Precepts of the Church

The precepts of the Church are laws that name specific actions that all Catholics are obligated to carry out.

1. Take part in the Mass on Sundays and holy days. Keep these days holy and avoid unnecessary work.
2. Celebrate the Sacrament of Reconciliation at least once a year if there is serious sin.
3. Receive Holy Communion at least once a year during Easter time.
4. Fast and/or abstain on days of penance.
5. Give your time, gifts, and money to support the Church.

Faith Fact

Pope Benedict XVI was born Joseph Ratzinger on April 16, 1927, in Marktl am Inn, Germany. He was ordained a priest in 1951. He later became a bishop, and then Cardinal in 1977. The College of Cardinals selected him to be Pope in 2005. He was a close confidant of his predecessor, John Paul II, and presided over his funeral.

Prayer

The Apostles' Creed

I believe in God, the Father almighty,
creator of heaven and earth.
I believe in Jesus Christ, his only Son,
    our Lord.
He was conceived by the power of the Holy Spirit,
and born of the Virgin Mary.
He suffered under Pontius Pilate,
was crucified, died, and was buried.
He descended to the dead.
On the third day, he rose again.
He ascended into heaven,
and is seated at the right hand of
    the Father.
He will come again to judge the living
    and the dead.
I believe in the Holy Spirit,
the holy Catholic Church,
the communion of saints,
the forgiveness of sins,
the resurrection of the body,
and the life everlasting. Amen.

Faith Fact

When a pope is elected, he is given a ring with a figure of Saint Peter fishing on it. This reminds the pope that he is to be a leader of God's people as Peter was.

Fathers of the Church

Apostolic fathers were first- and second-century Christian writers who give us information about the early Christian Church. They are called *apostolic* because it is believed they had a historical connection to the Apostles. Saints Clement, Ignatius of Antioch, and Polycarp, the author of *The Epistle of Barnabas* and the *Didache*, which includes several important teachings of the early Church, are considered apostolic fathers. Saints Athanasius, Basil, Gregory of Nazianzus, John Chrysostom, Ambrose, Augustine, Gregory, Jerome, Justin Martyr, Irenaeus, and Cyprian are called **fathers of the Church** because of some of their great writings and teachings.

Patriarchs of the Old Testament

The term *patriarch* refers to the male ancestors of Israel who appear in the Book of Genesis both before and after the flood. The most significant patriarchs are Abraham, Isaac, and Jacob.

Life after Death

- The **particular judgment** is the judgment made at the moment of a person's death. At this judgment the soul is rewarded with the blessings of heaven, given a time of purification, or condemned to hell.
- **Heaven** is the state of being happy with God forever.
- **The final purification (purgatory)** is a time after death for those who are in God's friendship but need to be purified to be with him in heaven.
- **Hell** is the state of separation from God forever.
- The **last judgment** is also called the general judgment. God, in the person of the glorified Christ, will judge the moral quality of each person's life. He will also show how God's justice has defeated all the injustice of humans in history.
- The **new heaven and new earth** is the kingdom of God (or new Jerusalem) that will come in its fullness at the end of time.

Creed

Faith Fact

When a religious work is ready for publication, it is submitted to a bishop for approval. If approved, it is given an imprimatur. This means that it is free from any doctrinal error.

Rev. Peter Klein, *The Catholic Source Book.*

Ecumenism

Ecumenism is a movement that seeks to bring about the unity of all Christian churches. The word *ecumenism* comes from a scriptural phrase in Greek that means "the whole household of God."

Canonization of Saints

Saints are very holy people who committed their lives to God. The Church uses a process called canonization to declare a person a saint.

Steps of Canonization

A person or group of people approach their bishop to suggest a candidate for sainthood. A committee creates a report on the candidate and sends it to the Congregation for the Causes of Saints.

1. The Congregation researches the candidate to verify that he or she practiced virtue. When the pope accepts the Congregation's report, the candidate is termed "venerable," or "servant of God."

2. The second process is a very lengthy research of the life of the candidate. A "promoter of the cause" is authorized to examine the person's life, virtues, writings, reputation for holiness, and reported miracles. As a rule one miracle must be credited to the candidate's intercession with God. The venerable candidate is then "beatified" by the pope. The person is designated as "blessed."

3. Canonization is the solemn declaration by the pope that the candidate is a saint. This declaration requires one more miracle.

Liturgical Year

The liturgical year is the Church's annual cycle of seasons and feasts that celebrates the Paschal mystery. It begins on the First Sunday of Advent and ends on the feast of Christ the King. This feast honors Jesus' reign over all of heaven and earth. It affirms the messianic kingship of Christ who gave his life through his death on the cross.

Ordinary Time is the name given to the thirty-three or thirty-four weeks during the year apart from the Seasons of Advent, Christmas, Lent, and Easter. The term *ordinary* comes from the Latin word *ordinis* which means "number." The Sundays of Ordinary Time are numbered consecutively. They are divided into two groups. The first group marks the time between Christmas and Lent. The second group marks the time between Easter and Advent. Ordinary Time celebrates the fullness of the Christian mystery. The Scripture readings for this time are about the words and actions of Jesus in his public life. They call members of the Church to discipleship. The liturgical color for Ordinary Time is green.

Holy Days of Obligation

Catholics are required to attend Mass on Sunday unless a serious reason prevents them from doing so. Catholics also must go to Mass on certain holy days. In the United States the holy days of obligation are the feasts of:

- Mary the Mother of God (January 1)
- the Ascension of the Lord (forty days after Easter or the Sunday nearest the end of the forty-day period)
- the Assumption of Mary (August 15)
- All Saints' Day (November 1)
- the Immaculate Conception of Mary (December 8)
- Christmas (December 25)

Order of the Mass

Introductory Rites
- Sign of the Cross and Greeting
- Rite of Blessing and Sprinkling Rite or Penitential Rite
- Glory to God (Gloria)
- Opening Prayer

Liturgy of the Word
- First Reading
- Responsorial Psalm
- Second Reading
- Gospel Acclamation
- Proclamation of the Gospel
- Homily
- Profession of Faith
- General Intercessions

Liturgy of the Eucharist
- Preparation of the Altar and the Gifts
- Eucharistic Prayer
- Preface
- Thanks and praise for God's great works
- Holy, Holy, Holy Lord (Sanctus)
- Calling on the Holy Spirit
- Consecration of bread and wine
- Memorial Acclamation
- Offering the Eucharistic sacrifice to God
- Prayers for the living and the dead
- Doxology and Great Amen

Communion Rite
- Lord's Prayer
- Sign of Peace
- Breaking of Bread
- Invitation to Communion
- Communion and Communion Song
- Period of Silence or Song of Praise
- Prayer After Communion

Concluding Rite
- Greeting
- Blessing and dismissal

Faith Fact

It is common in Latin America for the Last Supper to be reenacted in church during Triduum. The presiding priest and twelve men—dressed as Jesus and the disciples—dramatize or act out the Last Supper as recorded in the Gospel.

Rev. Peter Klein, *The Catholic Source Book.*

Devotions

Novena

A novena is a private devotion. The word *novena* comes from the Latin word *novem* which means "nine." A novena is a prayer in honor of one of the three Persons of the Holy Trinity, the Blessed Virgin Mary, or one of the saints that is repeated over the course of nine days, weeks, or months for a special intention.

Stations of the Cross

The devotional practice of the Stations of the Cross began in the early Church. Pilgrims would visit the various sites in Jerusalem that were associated with Christ's suffering and death. The Stations of the Cross focus on fourteen scenes of Christ's Passion.

First Station: Jesus is condemned to death on the cross.
Second Station: Jesus accepts his cross.
Third Station: Jesus falls the first time.
Fourth Station: Jesus meets his sorrowful mother.
Fifth Station: Simon of Cyrene helps Jesus carry his cross.
Sixth Station: Veronica wipes the face of Jesus.
Seventh Station: Jesus falls the second time.
Eighth Station: Jesus meets and speaks to the women of Jerusalem.
Ninth Station: Jesus falls the third time.
Tenth Station: Jesus is stripped of his garments.
Eleventh Station: Jesus is nailed to the cross.
Twelfth Station: Jesus dies on the cross.
Thirteenth Station: Jesus is taken down from the cross.
Fourteenth Station: Jesus is placed in the tomb.

Moral Law

There are four expressions of moral law:

1. Divine law is the plan of God's wisdom to direct all human activity to good.
2. Natural moral law is the law that is written in your heart that helps you know what is good and what is evil.
3. Revealed law is law as it is revealed in the Old and New Testaments.
4. Civil and Church laws are established by nations and by the Church to promote the common good and to guide the decisions of each person.

Ten Commandments

1. I am the Lord your God. You shall not have strange gods before me.
2. You shall not take the name of the Lord your God in vain.
3. Remember to keep holy the Lord's day.
4. Honor your father and your mother.
5. You shall not kill.
6. You shall not commit adultery.
7. You shall not steal.
8. You shall not bear false witness against your neighbor.
9. You shall not covet your neighbor's wife.
10. You shall not covet your neighbor's goods.

The Great Commandment

"You shall love the Lord your God with all your heart, with all your soul, with all your strength, with all your mind; and your neighbor as yourself."

Luke 10:27

The Beatitudes

The Beatitudes are the promises of blessing made by Jesus to those who faithfully follow his example. They give direction to the human heart for finding the happiness that can be found in God alone. They teach about God's kingdom and the participation in eternal life to which all are called.

Blessed are the poor in spirit,
  for theirs is the kingdom of heaven.
Blessed are they who mourn,
  for they will be comforted.
Blessed are the meek,
  for they will inherit the land.
Blessed are they who hunger and thirst for righteousness,
  for they will be satisfied.
Blessed are the merciful,
  for they will be shown mercy.
Blessed are the clean of heart,
  for they will see God.
Blessed are the peacemakers,
  for they will be called children of God.
Blessed are they who are persecuted for the sake of
  righteousness,
  for theirs is the kingdom of heaven.

Matthew 5:3–10

Gifts and Fruits of the Holy Spirit

Wisdom	Right judgment (*Counsel*)
Understanding	Courage (*Fortitude*)
Knowledge	Reverence (*Piety*)
	Wonder and awe (*Fear of the Lord*)

Charity	Kindness	Faithfulness
Joy	Goodness	Modesty
Peace	Generosity	Self-control
Patience	Gentleness	Chastity

Grace

Grace is the free gift of God's presence in your life. Actual grace is the gift God gives you to do good and avoid evil. Sanctifying grace is a sharing in the life of God.

Faith Fact

Saint Joseph is the patron of peace, a happy home, and charity to people who are poor. His feast day is March 19. For Sicilians this feast is the occasion for hospitality. The tradition includes inviting to the table all who come to the door. A statue of Saint Joseph, surrounded by flowers and candles, is placed on the table as a centerpiece. A priest blesses the food. Any food brought by guests is offered to people who are poor.

Rev. Peter Klein, *The Catholic Source Book.*

Human Dignity

Human dignity means all humans have worth because they are made in the image of God. Because of human dignity, people have basic human rights, such as food, clothing, and shelter. No government or social group should fail to recognize those rights.

Justice and Peace

Justice is a cardinal virtue. It is the habit of always giving to everyone what is rightfully due them. Social justice is a part of this cardinal virtue. It is the part that urges individuals to seek the common good of the whole group rather than just his or her individual good.

Peace is a state of ordered tranquility. In the Catholic tradition peace is not just the absence of conflict. It is the result of right relationships with God and with your neighbor.

Common Good

The common good means all the conditions that allow people to become who God wants them to become. The common good includes peace, development of groups of people, and respect for every person. These conditions vary from society to society, which is why the Church does not recommend any one country's political or economic system. The Church evaluates each system on the basis of whether or not it provides the conditions for human fulfillment.

Sin

Sin is a choice to disobey God. It is a deliberate choice, not a mistake or an accident.

Sin is original or personal. Original sin is the sin committed by the first humans; all humans are born with this sin. Personal sins are personally chosen sins. They are either mortal or venial.

- **Mortal sin** breaks your relationship with God. For a sin to be mortal, three conditions must be present: It must be a serious matter. You must understand what you are going to do (sufficient reflection). You must fully agree to do it (full consent of the act).

Faith Fact

Paul the VI said, "If you want peace, work for justice."

Pius XII's motto was "Peace is the work of justice."

John XXIII showed his concern for the relationship between peace and justice in the encyclical *Peace on Earth*.

John Paul II said, "Peace is the work of solidarity."

- **Venial sin** hurts your relationship with God without breaking it. The effects of venial sin include a lessening of the love of God in your heart and a weakening of the power to resist sin.

  There are seven vices that the Church calls **capital sins**. They are also called the seven deadly sins. They are tendencies in a person that can lead to sin. The seven capital sins are pride, covetousness (desire), lust, anger, gluttony, envy, and sloth.

Virtues

Theological Virtues

Faith   Hope
Love

Cardinal Virtues

Prudence   Fortitude
Justice   Temperance

Works of Mercy

Corporal

Feed the hungry.
Give drink to the thirsty.
Clothe the naked.
Shelter the homeless.
Visit the sick.
Visit the imprisoned.
Bury the dead.

Spiritual

Warn the sinner.
Teach the ignorant.
Counsel the doubtful.
Comfort the sorrowful.
Bear wrongs patiently.
Forgive injuries.
Pray for the living and the dead.

Faith Fact

The rose has thorns as a reminder to humankind of the sin committed by the first humans and their fall from God's grace. The rose's beauty and fragrance remain as a reminder of paradise. The rose is also a symbol of Mary, the new Eve, the rose without thorns.

Rev. Peter Klein,
The Catholic Source Book.

Prayer

Faith Fact

A litany is a prayer consisting of a series of petitions prayed by a leader and responses by the group. Litanies have been part of the Christian tradition and can also be found in the Jewish tradition. One of the most popular litanies is the Litany of the Saints. It is used at the Easter Vigil and at ordination ceremonies.

The Lord's Prayer (Scriptural)

Our Father in heaven,
   hallowed be your name,
   your kingdom come,
   your will be done,
      on earth as in heaven.
Give us today our daily bread;
   and forgive us our debts,
      as we forgive our debtors;
   and do not subject us to the final test,
      but deliver us from the evil one.

Matthew 6:9–13

Hail Mary

Hail, Mary, full of grace,
   the Lord is with you!
Blessed are you among women,
   and blessed is the fruit of your womb, Jesus.
Holy Mary, Mother of God,
   pray for us sinners,
   now and at the hour of our death.
Amen.

Glory to the Father (Doxology)

Glory to the Father
and to the Son
and to the Holy Spirit: as it was in the beginning,
is now, and will be for ever.
Amen.

Jesus Prayer

Lord Jesus Christ, Son of God, have mercy on me, a sinner.

The Nicene Creed

We believe in one God,
   the Father, the Almighty,
   maker of heaven and earth,
   of all that is seen and unseen.
We believe in one Lord, Jesus Christ,
   the only Son of God,
   eternally begotten of the Father,
   God from God, Light from Light,
   true God from true God,
   begotten, not made,
   one in Being with the Father.
   Through him all things were made.
   For us men and for our salvation
   he came down from heaven:
   by the power of the Holy Spirit
   he was born of the Virgin Mary,
   and became man.
For our sake he was crucified
   under Pontius Pilate;
   he suffered, died, and was buried.
   On the third day he rose again
   in fulfillment of the Scriptures;
   he ascended into heaven
   and is seated at the right hand
   of the Father.

He will come again in glory
   to judge the living and the dead,
   and his kingdom will have no end.
We believe in the Holy Spirit,
   the Lord, the giver of life,
   who proceeds from the Father and the
   Son.
   With the Father and the Son
   he is worshiped and glorified.
   He has spoken through the Prophets.
   We believe in one holy
   catholic and apostolic Church.
   We acknowledge one baptism
   for the forgiveness of sins.
   We look for the resurrection of the dead,
   and the life of the world to come.
Amen.

Act of Faith

O God, we firmly believe that you are one God in three
divine Persons, Father, Son, and Holy Spirit; we believe that
your divine Son became man and died for our sins, and that
he will come to judge the living and the dead. We believe
these and all the truths that the holy Catholic Church teaches
because you have revealed them, and you can neither deceive
nor be deceived.

Faith Fact

Peace is often represented as a dove with an olive branch in its mouth. This comes from the Bible story of the great flood. When the dove Noah sent out from the ark returned with an olive branch, Noah knew the flood has ended. People were reconciled with God. The dove is also a sign of the Holy Spirit, whose gift to us is peace.

Act of Contrition

My God,
I am sorry for my sins with all my heart.
In choosing to do wrong
    and failing to do good,
I have sinned against you
    whom I should love above all things.
    I firmly intend, with your help,
    to do penance,
    to sin no more,
    and to avoid whatever leads me to sin.
Our Savior Jesus Christ
    suffered and died for us.
In his name, my God, have mercy.

The Canticle of Zechariah

Blessed be the Lord, the God of Israel;
he has come to his people and set them free.

He has raised up for us a mighty savior,
born of the house of his servant David.

Through his holy prophets he promised of old
    that he would save us from our enemies,
    from the hands of all who hate us.

He promised to show mercy to our fathers
and to remember his holy covenant.

This was the oath he swore to our father Abraham:
to set us free from the hands of our enemies,
free to worship him without fear,
holy and righteous in his sight
    all the days of our life.

Based on Luke 1:68–75

The Magnificat (Mary's Canticle)

My soul proclaims the greatness of the Lord,
my spirit rejoices in God my Savior;
for he has looked with favor on his lowly servant.
From this day all generations will call me blessed:
the Almighty has done great things for me,
and holy is his Name.
He has mercy on those who fear him
in every generation.
He has shown the strength of his arm,
he has scattered the proud in their conceit.
He has cast down the mighty from their thrones,
and has lifted up the lowly.
He has filled the hungry with good things,
and the rich he has sent away empty.
He has come to the help of his servant Israel
for he has remembered his promise of mercy,
the promise he made to our fathers,
to Abraham and his children for ever.

Based on Luke 1:46–55

Blessing Before Meals

Bless us, O Lord, and these your gifts
which we are about to receive
from your bounty
through Christ our Lord. Amen.

Thanksgiving After Meals

We give you thanks for all your gifts,
almighty God,
living and reigning now and forever. Amen.

Morning Prayer

I arise today
through God's strength to pilot me,
God's might to uphold me,
God's wisdom to guide me,
God's eye to look before me,
God's ear to hear me,
God's hand to guard me,
God's way to lie before me,
God's shield to protect me,
God's hosts to save me from the
    snares of the devil.

Saint Patrick's Breastplate

Faith Fact

We begin each day and end each day with prayer. We pray daily as a way to thank God for his many gifts. We talk to God and listen to his will. We also say a prayer at mealtime. We call this "saying grace." We thank God for giving us food to eat. We ask him to bless the food, and we remember people who don't have enough to eat.

Grace at Mealtime

Blessed are you, Lord.
You have fed us from our earliest days.
You give food to every living creature.
Fill our hearts with joy and delight.
Let us always have enough
and something to spare
for works of mercy
in honor of Christ Jesus, our Lord.
Through Christ may glory, honor, and power
be yours forever and ever. Amen.

Evening Prayer

Lord, from the rising of the sun to its
setting your name is worthy of all praise.
Let our prayer come like incense before
you. May the lifting up of our hands be
as an evening sacrifice acceptable to you,
Lord our God. Amen.

Prayer to the Holy Spirit

V. Come Holy Spirit, fill the hearts of
your faithful.
R. And kindle in them the fire of your love.
V. Send forth your Spirit and they shall be created.
R. And you will renew the face of the earth.

Prayer of Saint Francis

Lord, make me an instrument of your peace;
where there is hatred, let me sow love;
where there is injury, pardon;
where there is doubt, faith;
where there is despair, hope;
where there is darkness, light;
and where there is sadness, joy.

O divine Master, grant that I may not so much
seek
to be consoled as to console,
to be understood as to understand,
to be loved as to love;
for it is in giving that we receive,
it is in pardoning that we are pardoned,
and it is in dying that we are born to eternal life.
Amen.

Faith Fact

Personal prayer leads to public prayer, and public prayer leads to personal prayer. Prayer binds the person to God and God to that person. The connection from the person to God is Christ, the Son of God.

Act of Hope

O God, relying on your almighty power and your endless mercy and promises, we hope to gain pardon for our sins, the help of your grace, and life everlasting, through the saving actions of Jesus Christ, our Lord and Redeemer.

Act of Love

O God, we love you above all things, with our whole heart and soul, because you are all good and worthy of all love. We love our neighbor as ourselves for the love of you. We forgive all who have injured us and ask pardon of all whom we have injured.

Elements of the Lord's Prayer

The Lord's Prayer is made up of the following parts: praise, hope (a yearning for the kingdom of God), petition (asking for our needs to be met, and for forgiveness of sins), and a desire for goodness (freedom from testing or evil). There are actually seven petitions in this prayer.

The Seven Petitions of the Lord's Prayer	
Hallowed be thy name. Thy kingdom come. Thy will be done on earth as it is in heaven.	May your name be held holy. The first three petitions are more theological. They draw us toward the Father's glory, are for God's sake (thy name, thy kingdom, thy will), and are already answered in Jesus' sacrifice.
Give us this day our daily bread. Forgive us our trespasses, as we forgive those who trespass against us. Lead us not into temptation. Deliver us from evil.	Give us the food we need. Forgive us of our sins, as we will forgive those who sin against us. The last four ask God for improvement in our human situation. With them we put our weaknesses and our poverty of spirit in his hands. We gain strength and richness of spirit in his grace (give us, forgive us, lead us not, deliver us).

Eternal Rest

Eternal rest grant to them, O Lord,
and let perpetual light shine upon them.
May they rest in peace.
Amen.

Vocational Guidance

Dear God,
We know the love that you have for each of us.
We pray today that we keep an open heart and mind
and hear you when you are calling us.
May we be willing to listen,
and have the courage to respond.
If we ourselves are not called to religious life,
help us support and encourage those who are.
We pray for them in a special way.
Amen.

Angelus

V. The angel spoke God's message to Mary,
R. and she conceived of the Holy
    Spirit.
Hail, Mary . . .

V. "I am the lowly servant of the Lord:
R. let it be done to me according to your word."
Hail, Mary . . .

V. And the Word became flesh,
R. and lived among us.
Hail, Mary . . .

V. Pray for us, holy Mother of God,
R. that we may become worthy of the
promises of Christ.

Let us pray.

Lord,
fill our hearts with your grace:
once, through the message of an angel
you revealed to us the incarnation of
    your Son;
now, through his suffering and death
lead us to the glory of his resurrection.

We ask this through Christ our Lord.
Amen.

Faith Fact

The *Angelus* is a prayer honoring the Incarnation. It is given its name by the first word of the Latin version of the prayer: *Angelus Domini nuntiavit Maria*, "The angel of the Lord declared unto Mary." To honor the Incarnation, it is recited three times each day—morning, noon, and evening, at the sound of the *Angelus* bell. Each response, where shown, is followed by reciting the Hail Mary.

The Way of the Cross

The First Station: Jesus is condemned to death. *John 3:16*
"For God so loved the world that he gave his only Son, so that everyone who believes in him may not perish but may have eternal life."

The Second Station: Jesus bears his cross. *Luke 9:23*
"Then he said to them all, 'If any want to become my followers, let them deny themselves and take up their cross daily and follow me.'"

The Third Station: Jesus falls the first time. *Isaiah 53:6*
"All we like sheep have gone astray; we have all turned to our own way, and the Lord has laid on him the iniquity of us all."

The Fourth Station: Jesus meets his mother. *Lamentations 1:12*
"Is it nothing to you, all you who pass by? Look and see if there is any sorrow like my sorrow…"

The Fifth Station: Simon of Cyrene helps Jesus carry his cross. *Matthew 25:40*
"And the king will answer them, 'Truly I tell you, just as you did it to one of the least of these who are members of my family, you did it to me.'"

The Sixth Station: Veronica wipes the face of Jesus. *John 14:9*
"… 'Whoever has seen me has seen the Father'…"

The Seventh Station: Jesus falls a second time. *Matthew 11:28*
"Come to me, all you that are weary and are carrying heavy burdens, and I will give you rest."

The Eighth Station: Jesus meets the women of Jerusalem. *Luke 23:28*
"But Jesus turned to them and said, 'Daughters of Jerusalem, do not weep for me, but weep for yourselves and for your children.'"

The Ninth Station: Jesus falls a third time. *Luke 14:11*
"For all who exalt themselves will be humbled, and those who humble themselves will be exalted."

The Tenth Station: Jesus is stripped of his garments. *Luke 14:33*
"So therefore, none of you can become my disciple if you do not give up all your possessions."

The Eleventh Station: Jesus is nailed to the cross. *John 6:38*
"[F]or I have come down from heaven, not to do my own will, but the will of him who sent me."

The Twelfth Station: Jesus dies on the cross. *Philippians 2:7–8*
"...And being found in human form, he humbled himself and became obedient to the point of death—even death on a cross."
The Thirteenth Station: Jesus is taken down from the cross. *Luke 24:26*
"Was it not necessary that the Messiah should suffer these things and then enter into his glory?"
The Fourteenth Station: Jesus is placed in the tomb. *John 12:24*
"[Very truly, I tell you,] unless a grain of wheat falls into the earth and dies, it remains just a single grain; but if it dies, it bears much fruit."

Memorare

Remember, most loving Virgin Mary,
never was it heard
that anyone who turned to you for help
was left unaided.

Inspired by this confidence,
though burdened by my sins,
I run to your protection
for you are my mother.

Mother of the Word of God,
do not despise my words of pleading
but be merciful and hear my prayer.
Amen.

How to Pray the Rosary

1. Pray the Sign of the Cross and say the Apostles' Creed.
2. Pray the Lord's Prayer.
3. Pray three Hail Marys.
4. Pray the Glory to the Father.
5. Say the first mystery; then pray the Lord's Prayer.
6. Pray ten Hail Marys while meditating on the mystery.
7. Pray the Glory to the Father.
8. Say the second mystery; then pray the Lord's Prayer. Repeat 6 and 7 and continue with the third, fourth, and fifth mysteries in the same manner.
9. Pray the Hail, Holy Queen.

Faith Fact

As the Mother of Jesus, the Son of God, Mary is called the Mother of God, the Queen of all Saints, and the Mother of the Church. There are many prayers and practices of devotion to Mary. One of the most popular is the Rosary. It focuses on the twenty mysteries that describe events in the lives of Jesus and Mary.

The Mysteries of the Rosary

The Joyful Mysteries	The Luminous Mysteries
The Annunciation	The Baptism of Jesus
The Visitation	The Wedding at Cana
The Nativity	The Proclamation of the Kingdom
The Presentation in the Temple	The Transfiguration
The Finding in the Temple	The Institution of the Eucharist
The Sorrowful Mysteries	**The Glorious Mysteries**
The Agony in the Garden	The Resurrection
The Scourging at the Pillar	The Ascension
The Crowning with Thorns	The Descent of the Holy Spirit
The Carrying of the Cross	The Assumption of Mary
The Crucifixion and Death	The Coronation of Mary in Heaven

Hail, Holy Queen

Hail, holy Queen, Mother of mercy,
hail, our life, our sweetness, and our hope.
To you we cry, the children of Eve;
to you we send up our sighs,
mourning and weeping in this land of exile.
Turn, then, most gracious advocate,
your eyes of mercy toward us;
lead us home at last
and show us the blessed fruit of your womb,
  Jesus:
O clement, O loving, O sweet Virgin Mary.

Salve, Regina

Holy, Holy, Holy Lord

In English

Holy, holy, holy Lord, God of power and might,
heaven and earth are full of your glory.
Hosanna in the highest.

Blessed is he who comes in the name of the Lord.
Hosanna in the highest.

In Latin

Sanctus, Sanctus, Sanctus
Dominus Deus Sabaoth.
Pleni sunt coeli et terra gloria tua.
Hosanna in excelsis.

Benedictus qui venit in nomine Domini.
Hosanna in excelsis.

Lamb of God

In English

Lamb of God, you take away the
  sins of the world:
    have mercy on us.
Lamb of God, you take away the
  sins of the world:
    have mercy on us.
Lamb of God, you take away the
  sins of the world:
    grant us peace.

In Latin

Agnus Dei, qui tollis peccata mundi:
miserere nobis.
Agnus Dei, qui tollis peccata mundi:
miserere nobis.
Agnus Dei, qui tollis peccata mundi:
dona nobis pacem

Faith Fact

As members of the Catholic Church, we usually pray in the language that we speak, but we sometimes pray in Latin, the common language of the Church. The following are a couple of the common prayers of the Church in both English and Latin.

249

Faith in Action!
CATHOLIC SOCIAL TEACHING

Faith in Action!
CATHOLIC SOCIAL TEACHING

Care for Creation

Like all the beautiful things on earth, flowers are a gift of God the Creator. Gratitude to him is an appropriate response to their beauty. As one of God's stewards, you can help care for this natural beauty. By planting gardens, humans cooperate with God in making the world more beautiful. They act as good caretakers of creation.

God has provided all the resources that allow humans to lead rich and comfortable lives: the air they breathe and the water they drink, the soil and the plants that grow in it, the minerals under the ground, the animals, birds, insects, and fish. He wants humans to show their thankfulness for all of these resources by using them wisely and ensuring that they remain available for future generations.

❓ **Why is it necessary for humans to cooperate with God to preserve the earth's varied resources?**

Mary's Gardens

As a part of God's creation, flowers show the beauty and wonder of God. Let's look at what one organization did to care for God's special gift of flowers.

Centuries ago, Catholics in England honored Jesus' mother, the Virgin Mary, by giving to hundreds of common flowers names that reminded them of her. For example, the larkspur, a plant that produces many small blooms growing on long spikes, was once named "Mary's tears." The morning glory, a large flower with blue and white stripes, was called "Our Lady's mantle." The original name of the shiny yellow marigold was "Mary gold." So many different kinds of flowers were named after Mary that you could have a whole garden full of them—and many people did. These gardens were called Mary Gardens.

In the seventeenth century, the English Puritans discouraged devotion to Mary and the saints. They also discouraged people from planting Mary Gardens and even from using the Mary names for flowers. Soon most of these names were forgotten.

In recent times in the United States, the custom of planting Mary Gardens has been revived. In 1951 John Stokes and Edward McTague, two American Catholics, started an organization in Philadelphia, Pennsylvania, called Mary's Gardens. By reading old books, members of this organization have rediscovered dozens of forgotten flower names relating to Mary and other saints. Thanks to the organization's efforts, Mary Gardens have been planted throughout the world on the grounds of schools, parishes, monasteries, and shrines, as well as in people's yards.

? How do Mary Gardens help care for God's creation?

Reach Out!

Displaying God's Creation

Every patch of the earth, including the neighborhood in which you live, belongs to God. You have an opportunity to make your own neighborhood a beautiful garden for God.

List one or two simple things you can do to make your neighborhood look more pleasing to God and to the people who live there.

_____

_____

_____

Make a Difference

Plan a Neighborhood Project   Discuss ideas with your class as to how you can carry out a neighborhood improvement project. Together, decide on one project that the group can plan and carry out.

_____

1. Specific tasks that need to be done to carry out the project:

_____

2. Equipment required to do the project:

_____

3. Specific task assigned to you:

_____

4. Calendar for the project:

_____

DISCOVER

Catholic Social
Teaching:

Life and Dignity
of the Human
Person

Faith in Action!
CATHOLIC SOCIAL TEACHING

Life and Dignity

It is important to respect the life and dignity of each person. Because all humans are created in the image of God, everyone has value and worth, including those who are in prison.

Comforting those in prison is one of the seven Corporal Works of Mercy. Jesus singled out care for those who are in prison in one of his parables when he said, "... just as you did it to one of the least of these who are members of my family, you did to me" (*Matthew 25:40*).

In Jesus' time, there were surely people in prison who were innocent of the crimes of which they were accused, just as there are today. In his parable, however, Jesus did not say that God would bless people for visiting or writing to prisoners only if these prisoners were innocent. It is a blessed action to comfort anyone who is in jail, even if that person has committed a dreadful crime. A prisoner has the dignity that belongs to a person created by God. God loves the prisoner as he loves every person he has made.

What is true of prisoners is true of persons who are sick, persons with serious disabilities, and persons who are still unborn. The value and dignity of every human life is a basic teaching of the Catholic Church.

? **What actions do you perform to show that you respect the dignity of other people?**

A Loving Voice from Outside

God calls his followers to respect the life and dignity of all human persons. Let's look at how one organization put these beliefs into action.

Today more than one million men and women are in America's jails and prisons. Several thousand of these people have been condemned to death. They are often kept in a special part of the prison known as "death row." Usually many years pass between the trial at which they are sentenced to die and the actual date of execution. While these prisoners wait, they are often lonely.

In 1977, after a ten-year halt, the Supreme Court gave each state the right to adopt the death penalty. In response, Rachel and Bob Gross founded a ministry called the Death Row Support Project. The idea was to put prisoners on death row in touch with people outside who were willing to be pen pals with the prisoners. The letters the prisoners received would provide a friendly link to the outside world. The prisoners would be assured that they were not forgotten. Many people throughout the country have become pen pals with prisoners through this ministry.

? How do letters sent to death row inmates help promote respect for the life and dignity of the human person?

255

Reach Out!

Communicate with the Lonely

Being a pen pal for someone in prison is a very serious adult commitment. But remember that there are many other people in the world who are also lonely and suffering. They, too, would welcome a friendly letter from you.

What sorts of people might especially value a friendly letter?

_____

_____

_____

Think about the kind of letter you would write to one of these lonely people.

What are some appropriate things that you might say or discuss in the letter? How can you use your letter to affirm the person's dignity as one created in the image and likeness of God?

_____

_____

_____

_____

What are some things to avoid saying in order not to hurt the person's feelings?

_____

_____

_____

_____

_____

Make a Difference

Write a Letter Gather together in a group. With your teacher's help, decide what sort of person will receive your letters. Discuss your ideas about appropriate things to say in your letters. Draw up a schedule so that each student knows when it will be his or her turn to write a letter.

DISCOVER

Catholic Social
Teaching:

Rights and
Responsibilities
of the Human
Person

Faith in Action!
CATHOLIC SOCIAL TEACHING

Rights and Responsibilities

Catholics are called to support the rights and responsibilities of all people. By doing so, the respect and dignity of every person is maintained. It is everyone's responsibility to reach out to others and to help those who are in need.

Those who are poor face hunger and cold. But there are many other things about being poor that make life difficult. People who are poor often have to worry about not having enough money to meet all their needs. It is difficult for them to feel secure.

One of the basic teachings of the Church is that people have a right to a decent life—to food, clothing, housing, education, and medical care. They also have the right to a job, which provides independence, security, and self-respect.

All people share the responsibility of seeing to it that everyone is provided with these things.

? How are human rights and human responsibilities linked?

"Braking" the Cycle of Poverty

God calls his followers to protect the rights and responsibilities of the human person. Let's look at how one group of people put these beliefs into action.

In the summer of 2003, a group of thirty Catholics decided to do something spectacular to call attention to the problem of poverty in this country. They rode their bicycles across the United States. Twenty of them started out from California. Ten more started out later from Connecticut. The two groups arranged to meet in Baltimore, Maryland, and then ride together into the nation's capital, Washington, D.C. On the way they stopped in parishes in twelve states to talk to their fellow Catholics about poverty.

The riders named their project "Brake the Cycle of Poverty." The word *cycle* referred to the bicycles they rode. But the riders also had in mind a second meaning of the word *cycle*. A person who is poor needs a job so that he or she can make money to meet basic needs. However, a person often needs training, transportation, or new clothing so that he or she can go to a job interview. All of these things cost money—and where will that money come from?

What the Church wants to do is to "brake," or stop, the cycle of poverty. She wants to give those who are poor the skills and opportunities they need to climb out of poverty for good. This is what the riders talked about in the parishes that they visited.

❓ **What different kinds of help would you give to a poor family if you wanted to help the members move out of poverty for good?**

© Harcourt Religion

Reach Out!

Learning About Poverty

The Catholic bishops of the United States have set up a special office to fight poverty. It is called the Catholic Campaign for Human Development (CCHD). The CCHD has produced an impressive educational Web site about being poor in America, www.PovertyUSA.org.

Explore this Web site as a class. Then write down three facts you learned from the Web site that you think every Catholic should know.

If you do not have Internet access, you may want to visit your local library to find books and articles dealing with the subject of poverty or to use library computers for your research.

The three most interesting facts I learned were

_____

_____

_____

_____

_____

_____

Make a Difference

Give a Presentation The riders who took part in the "Brake the Cycle of Poverty" tour gave a presentation to the people at every parish where they stopped. You can help carry on their work. As a class, design a presentation about poverty in America, basing the presentation on facts you learned from the Poverty USA Web site. You will need to decide which facts are most important and how to present them. When you are ready, present what you have learned to another class in your school.

DISCOVER

Catholic Social
Teaching:

The Dignity of
Work and the
Rights of Workers

Faith in Action!
CATHOLIC SOCIAL TEACHING

The Dignity of Work

Work is not just a means of earning money. Through their labor, humans are in partnership with God in his work of creation. Work produces order, usefulness, and beauty. The work that people do should enhance their dignity.

Sometimes a worker is deprived of his or her dignity by an employer. Individual workers are often unable to negotiate their pay or working hours. They may be forced to work under conditions that endanger their health.

This is why workers form labor unions. Unions bargain with employers on behalf of all the workers in a particular factory or even in an entire industry. Solidarity in a labor union allows workers to ask that companies pay decent wages, maintain safe conditions at the work site, and give employees time off to be with their families.

For the past century, the Catholic Church throughout the world has strongly supported the right of workers to form unions because these organizations are a powerful force to help workers get the benefits necessary to live in dignity.

❓ **What are some things that make working enjoyable and pleasant for adults?**

A Priest for the Workers

Monsignor George Higgins was a priest from Illinois. In 1944 he took a "temporary" job in Washington, D.C. He began working for the National Catholic Welfare Conference, an organization founded by America's Catholic bishops to support the interests of working people in America.

The rights of workers are an important element in maintaining human worth and dignity. Let's look at how one man put this belief into action.

Higgins stayed at his "temporary" job for 36 years. He became the best-known defender of workers' rights in the American Catholic Church. He managed to get support from people all over America for the famous labor leader Cesar Chavez. Chavez wanted to form a union for the Mexican migrant workers in California who picked table grapes.

Starting in 1945, Monsignor Higgins wrote a newspaper column called "The Yardstick." It appeared regularly in Catholic papers all over the country and was written to address issues related to the labor movement. By the time he gave up writing in 2001, Higgins had written almost 3000 columns!

Monsignor Higgins spent his adult life defending one basic principle: the right of workers to join together in labor unions to defend their interests. Unions gave workers the power to receive raises in pay and improve the way their families lived. Unions also gave workers the means of influencing public policy, because lawmakers and other elected officials could not ignore the views of millions of working people represented by unions.

❓ How did Monsignor Higgins help the cause of labor unions?

**Catholic labor leader
Monsignor George C. Higgins**

Cesar Chavez (standing at left) shakes hands with a representative of California's grape growers after the signing of a new labor contract, while Monsignor Higgins (standing at far right) looks on.

The Yardstick

Rally for Reform of Immigrant Labor ws

By Msgr. George G. H

July 3, 2000
As many as 20
a host of lab
converged
call for ref
nesty fo
rtune to a
d its

261

Reach Out!

Unions Where I Live

Consult a local city's telephone directory. Look in the section titled "labor organizations" or "labor unions." You will find a list of unions that operate in your community or state. In the chart, write the name of the organization or union and what type of work its members do.

Organization or Union	Type of Work Performed

Make a Difference

Research an Occupation Choose one type of work from the chart. In the library or on the Internet, research the occupation you have selected. Then write a summary of your findings, explaining how the work done by people in this occupation is valuable to society. Report what you have learned to another class, to a group of parents, or to your local parish.

Faith in Action!
CATHOLIC SOCIAL TEACHING

Solidarity

The word *catholic* comes from two Greek words that mean "according to the whole." When the early Christians described their church as the *Catholic* Church, they meant that the Church extended throughout the known world and united people of every race and culture.

Solidarity is the unity that comes from recognizing that all of humanity is one family. It is a virtue that Catholics are called to practice in order to live up to the meaning of their name. Solidarity means recognizing that all men and women are brothers and sisters, whatever language they speak, whatever clothes they wear. When people anywhere experience injustice, you feel the hurt. When people are suffering, even if it is on the other side of the globe, you recognize a responsibility to help them.

What happens in the world today affects people everywhere. Thanks to airplanes, television, telephones, and the Internet, no place is really that far away from any other. You can learn about the suffering of people in many different places and offer them real help. In doing so, you can show solidarity with the whole human community.

> ❓ **What are some things that would bring greater solidarity to the world?**

From Minnesota to Kenya

Solidarity sees all humans as part of one global community. Let's look at how one American diocese practiced solidarity.

Minnesota is in the center of North America. It has long and bitterly cold winters. When you live in Minnesota, hot, dry East Africa seems very far away. But the Catholics who live in a diocese in Minnesota took the principle of solidarity quite seriously. Through Catholic Relief Services, America's leading Catholic aid organization, the people of the diocese forged a relationship with the people of a diocese in Kenya.

As it is in Minnesota, farming is one of the main occupations in Kenya. But many of the farmers there are very poor. When they talked to Catholic Relief Services, the farmers easily identified one reason for their poverty. Leaky wooden containers were all they had for storing their grain. Rats and insects could easily get into the containers and eat the grain. When it rained, the grain became moldy. As much as thirty percent of the crop was lost before it could be eaten or sold.

The Catholics of the diocese in Minnesota decided that a good way to help the Kenyans would be to supply them with strong metal silos for storing grain. But rather than simply buying silos and shipping them to Kenya, they paid for Kenyan craftsmen to be trained in the building of silos. The new silos built by the Kenyan people will last up to fifty years without much maintenance. And now that they have learned their trade, the craftsmen make a good income by producing silos for people all over Kenya.

❓ **Why was it better to teach Kenyans to build silos than to export silos from America?**

Reach Out!

Reflect on Solidarity

From what you have learned about solidarity, think of how you can practice solidarity in your own life. Use the Minnesota diocese as your model. In what ways can you promote greater unity in your family, in your school, in your community, and in the world? Write your ideas on the lines provided.

_____

_____

_____

_____

_____

_____

Make a Difference

Draw a Poster   Using words and pictures, design a poster illustrating the relationship of solidarity between the Minnesota diocese and the diocese in Kenya. Your sketch might include a drawing of a Kenyan village and its people; farmers with their new silos; the people in Minnesota; a drawing of the two bishops, American and Kenyan, standing together; and maps of Kenya and the United States. Display the class posters in a prominent place in the school.

DISCOVER

Catholic Social
Teaching:

Call to Family,
Community, and
Participation

Faith in Action!
CATHOLIC SOCIAL TEACHING

Call to Community

For some people, the only goal in life is to look after "number one" (themselves). They argue that they have no obligation to worry about anyone else's problems. They boast that they do not need anyone's help to get by.

This is not the way God intended human life to be lived. He planned for you to be born into a community, the family. It is there that you were first introduced to the faith and values that will sustain you through life.

God has also arranged to bring you salvation as a member of a larger community—the Church.

Communities like the family, the Church, and the country are precious. These communities form a framework that will enable you to lead a good life. In return, though, you have a duty to participate actively in these institutions. You need to accept responsibilities within your family, the Church, and the country in which you live.

❓ **What are some ways that a family helps society?**

Old and Young Together

In any community, it is important for young people to learn and share with people who are older and have much to offer society. Let's look at how one organization answered the call to participate within the community.

Linda Holloway lives in Colorado. Her grandmother Bessie lived in a care center in Texas. Every time she visited the center, Linda became more convinced that her grandmother was not getting the attention she needed and deserved.

After her grandmother died, Linda had an inspiration. She came up with a plan to bring joy and stimulation to older people who lead lonely lives in care centers. She and her friend Sharron Brandrup founded an organization called Rainbow Bridge. The purpose of Rainbow Bridge is to improve the lives of older people by bringing groups of young people into care centers to visit them. The older people help the young people with reading and other academic skills. They also tell wonderful stories about what life was like when they were young. In return, the young people offer love, companionship, and a chance to feel useful.

Rainbow Bridge programs have been a great success. More than 13,000 kids in Colorado and New Mexico have participated in the program. By building this bridge between the generations, the organization has enriched the lives of both young and old. When young people and older people are brought together, they often find that they have much in common.

? **What kinds of things do old and young people have in common?**

Reach Out!

Plan a Visit

Plan a visit to a local care center for older people. Decide in advance what sorts of things you are going to do to become involved in the lives of the center's residents. For example, you could lead a prayer service for them or sing for them. You might also arrange to play cards or a board game with the residents. Write your ideas here, and discuss them with the rest of the class.

_____

_____

_____

_____

Make a Difference

Visit a Care Center   Complete the planning checklist. After making all of the necessary preparations, go to the care center and carry out your plan.

Activity	Time Needed	People Involved	Location
example: Prayer Service	15 minutes	whole class	care center chapel

Faith in Action!
CATHOLIC SOCIAL TEACHING

Option for the Poor

Jesus challenged the beliefs of his society when he told those who were poor that they were blessed. His love for those who were disadvantaged both amazed and offended the rich and "respectable" people.

Every disciple of Jesus is called to love and serve those who are poor. As a Christian, you are called to examine your own life regularly to see whether you really *must* have everything you are tempted to buy. By denying yourself a few of these things, you can assist people who desperately need help.

Today's world is one of extremes. Tremendous wealth exists in many countries. However, extreme poverty exists in other countries. The Church insists that this situation is not morally acceptable. Recent popes have taught that rich countries have the same kind of responsibility to poor countries that people who are wealthy have to those who are poor.

? **What things can Americans do to relieve poverty elsewhere in the world?**

A Life of Charity

As a Christian, you are called to show love to others, including those who are poor. Let's look at how one woman and her many spiritual daughters showed love and care for those who were poor and vulnerable.

Mother Elizabeth Ann Seton was the first person born in the United States to be declared a saint by the Church. In 1809 she and four companions founded the Daughters of Charity of Saint Joseph. The Daughters of Charity established the first parochial school for girls, the first Catholic hospital, and the first Catholic orphanage in the United States.

The Daughters of Charity continue to provide loving service to people who are poor, sick, or both.

Today thirteen different communities of women take their inspiration from Saint Elizabeth Ann Seton. Together they have more than 5000 members. Mother Seton would surely approve of the work that they do. One sister runs a food pantry in Ohio. Another offers free medical care to poor people living on the U.S.–Mexican border. A third offers medical help and prayer to African villagers infected with AIDS. And a fourth, who lives in Nepal, rescues women with a history of mental illness from the jails in which they are often placed and gives them treatment in her clinic.

? What are some ways that the Daughters of Charity perform works of service for those who are poor and vulnerable?

Reach Out!

Help the Needy

Just as the Daughters of Charity carry out various works of love and service to help those who are poor and sick, all Christians have a responsibility to reach out to those in need.

Brainstorm with your classmates some ideas about how your class can raise money to help needy people in your community. Think of different people or groups that you can help. Think of possible fund-raisers, and set a goal of how much money you would like to give. Use the questions in the chart to help you brainstorm.

What charity or group can we help?	What are some possible fund-raising ideas?	What services can we do or what items can we sell?	How long will the fund-raiser last?	What is the amount of money we hope to raise?

Make a Difference

Raise Funds   Carry out the plan you have made for raising funds. After completing the fund-raiser, discuss the plan and its results as a class.

What did you learn from the fund-raiser about serving and helping those in need?

How will you continue to help those in need?

WORDS OF FAITH

A

---

anoint To use oil to mark someone as chosen for a special purpose. In biblical times, the priests, the kings, and sometimes the prophets were anointed as a sign of God's favor. *(95)*

apocalyptic literature A type of writing that claims to reveal what humans cannot see. *(215)*

apostolic A mark of the Church. The Church is apostolic because the teaching authority of the Church comes directly from Jesus and his chosen Apostles because the bishops of the Church are direct successors of the Apostles. *(139)*

apostolic succession The term used to describe how the authority and power to lead and teach the Church is passed down from the Apostles to their successors, the bishops. *(131)*

B

Beatitudes Teachings of Jesus that sum up the way to live in God's kingdom. They point the way to true happiness. *(148)*

Bible God's word written down by humans. It is the Church's holy book. *(43)*

C

---

catholic A mark of the Church. The Church is catholic because its mission is to the whole world. *(139)*

charism A special gift or grace of the Holy Spirit given to help a person live out the Christian life or serve the common good in building up the Church. *(183)*

charity The theological virtue of loving God above all things and loving your neighbor as yourself for the love of God. *(149)*

chastity A moral virtue and one of the fruits of the Holy Spirit. Chastity helps people express their sexuality in the right way for their call in life. *(183)*

chrism Blessed oil used for anointing in the Sacraments of Baptism, Confirmation, and Holy Orders. *(175)*

Church The community of all baptized people who believe in God and follow Jesus. *(123)*

communion of saints When referring to holy persons, the communion of saints includes the pilgrim Church on earth, those being purified in purgatory, and the blessed already in heaven. *(199)*

conscience A gift from God that helps you know the difference between right and wrong and helps you choose what is right. *(165)*

consecrated life A state of life lived in community and characterized by the vows of poverty, chastity, and obedience. *(183)*

covenant A sacred promise or agreement between humans or between God and humans. God made covenants with Noah, Abraham, and Moses in the Old Testament. In the New Testament Jesus' sacrifice established the new and everlasting covenant through his death and Resurrection. *(59)*

creed A formal statement of what is believed. The word *creed* comes from the Latin for "I believe." There are two main creeds of the Church: the Nicene Creed and the Apostles' Creed. *(139)*

D

Decalogue Another name for the Ten Commandments, laws that God gave Moses. The first three commandments have to do with the relationship between God and the people. The other seven commandments help people respect one another. *(85)*

72

denomination A religious group with its own organization, worship, and set of beliefs. *(208)*

dignity The inner worth due to persons because they are made in the image and likeness of God. *(155)*

domestic Church The family is called the domestic Church because it is the place where children first learn about God through the love, teaching, and good example of parents and other family members. *(191)*

ecumenism An organized effort to bring Christians together in cooperation as they look forward in hope to the restoration of the unity of the Christian Church. *(209)*

epistles Letters written by Paul and several of the other Apostles and disciples to new Christian communities that were established. There are twenty-one letters in the New Testament. *(137)*

eternity Time without end and new life beyond death. *(53)*

evangelize To give witness to the faith by proclaiming the good news of Jesus Christ to the world through words and actions. *(175)*

exile The time when Judah, the southern kingdom, was conquered by the Babylonians (586 B.C.). As a result, the people of Judah were sent into exile in Babylon, away from their homeland. *(111)*

Exodus The Israelites' journey from slavery in Egypt to freedom in the promised land, accomplished and directed by God. *(79)*

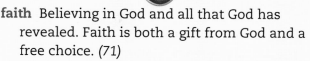

faith Believing in God and all that God has revealed. Faith is both a gift from God and a free choice. *(71)*

faithfulness The loyalty and steadfastness that God shows to all humans, even when they sin. God's offer of friendship is never withdrawn. *(59)*

fidelity Faithful presence. It is the most important rule of loving and lasting relationships. *(84)*

Genesis The first book of the Bible tells of God's creation of the world and his covenant with our ancestors in faith. *(52)*

gospel The good news of God's saving love. *(122)*

holy A mark of the Church. The Church is holy because God is holy. Christ gave himself up to make the Church holy and gave the Church the gift of the Holy Spirit to give it life. *(138)*

Holy Orders The Sacrament in which a man is ordained to serve the mission of Jesus and the Church as deacon, priest, or bishop. *(182)*

I

intercessory prayer A form of prayer in which you pray to God on behalf of another. *(201)*

J

justice To give God what is due him. It also means to give each person what he or she is due because that person is a child of God. *(155)*

L

Last Supper Jesus' celebration of the Passover meal with the Apostles. During this supper, Jesus turned the bread and wine into his Body and Blood. *(79)*

273

marks of the Church The essential characteristics that distinguish the Church and its mission. The Church is one, holy, catholic, and apostolic. (139)

martyr A saint or holy person who loses his or her life for following Jesus. The word *martyr* means "witness." (131)

Matrimony The Sacrament of Service in which a man and woman make a covenant of love with each other and with God. (189)

meditation A form of prayer in which you are attentive to God's presence in your life. (201)

messiah The promised one who would lead his people. The word *messiah* means "God's anointed," or "God's chosen one." (113)

ministry The work of service by ordained ministers and, in certain circumstances, by laypeople. (183)

mission For a Christian to be sent forth to share the good news of Jesus and God's kingdom. (173)

missionary One who is sent to proclaim the good news of God's kingdom to people in other places or distant lands. (131)

mortal sin A very serious sin by which someone turns completely away from God. The conditions of mortal sin are: the matter must be serious; the person must know the sinful action is serious; and the person must freely choose to do it. (162)

natural moral law The natural common sense that is written in your heart before you are born. The rules of the Decalogue reflect the natural moral law. (85)

new creation The future of justice, love, and peace promised by God, in which good will be rewarded and evil punished. (217)

new Jerusalem The name for the Church in the Book of Revelation. The image pictures the most beautiful city in God's new creation. The new Jerusalem is compared to a bride, and Jesus, the Lamb of God, to a bridegroom. (217)

New Testament The second part of the Bible. It is about the story of Jesus, his followers, and the early Church. (123)

obedience Submitting to the authority of God. The Fourth Commandment requires children to obey their parents. It is one of the vows of consecrated life. (183)

Old Testament The first part of the Bible. It is about the story of the Hebrew people before Jesus was born. (53)

one A mark of the Church. The Church is one because it acknowledges one Lord, confesses one faith, and is born of one Baptism. (138)

oral tradition A form of communication whereby important events and teachings are passed on by word of mouth. The Bible is composed of writings based on the oral traditions of the people. (43)

original sin The sin of the first humans and its effects on all humans. Sin and death are part of the human condition because of the first humans' choice. (61)

P

Passover The Jewish holy day that celebrates God's leading the Israelites out of slavery in Egypt. (79)

peace The state of tranquility or harmony in which people respect the dignity of others. (157)

poverty One of the vows of consecrated life. (183)

prayer Raising your mind and heart to God. In prayer you both listen and talk to God. (71)

precepts of the Church The laws given by Church authorities. They are the basic guidelines for spiritual growth. (149)

priesthood of the baptized Refers to Christ giving the faithful a share in his priesthood through Baptism and Confirmation. (174)

prophet A messenger from God who speaks the truth and calls the people to justice. (111)

Protestant Reformation A sixteenth-century religious separation from the Catholic Church that began with Martin Luther's preaching against errors he saw in the Church. (207)

psalms Poems and hymns that were first used in the liturgy of the Israelites. Today the psalms are also prayed and sung in the public prayer of the Church. (97)

purgatory A state of final purification after death and before heaven. (199)

revelation The process by which God makes himself known. The chief sources of revelation are Scripture and Tradition. (43)

righteous To act in accordance with God's will, free from guilt or sin. (217)

Sabbath The seventh day of the week in the Jewish calendar. It is still observed by Jews as a day of rest and prayer and worship. (121)

sacramental seal Refers to the rule that a priest is not to reveal anything he hears in confession. (165)

Sacraments of Service The sacraments of Holy Orders and Matrimony. They help build up the People of God. (189)

salvation The loving action of God's forgiveness of sins and the restoration of friendship with him brought by Jesus. (43)

schism A break or division. (207)

sin An offense against God as well as against reason, truth, and conscience. (59)

social sin The unjust structures that can occur as the result of personal sin. One person's sin can cause others to sin, and the sin can spread through a whole society. (157)

Spiritual Works of Mercy Actions that care for the spiritual needs of others. (201)

temptation An attraction to sin, those actions and omissions that go against right reason and against God's law. (61)

Ten Commandments The law that God gave Moses included the Ten Commandments. The first three commandments have to do with the relationship between God and people. The other seven commandments help people respect one another. (85)

Torah The name the Hebrews gave the first five books of the Bible. The Jews still use this term today. (85)

transfiguration The revelation of Jesus in glory to the Apostles Peter, James, and John. (147)

virtue a habit of doing good. There are three theological virtues—faith, hope, and love—and four cardinal virtues—prudence, justice, fortitude, and temperance. (155)

vocation A call to love and serve God and others. (181)

vows Promises made to God. Religious vows include the public profession of what is called the evangelical counsels: poverty, chastity, and obedience. (183)

wisdom A gift from God that helps you understand his purpose and plan for your life. (103)

Illustration Credits

Wendy Ackison 58, 59, 104; Paul Bachem 42; Nick Backes 102; Kevin Beilfuss 198; Michael Bonilla 50; Ron Croci 110; The Curator Collection Ltd. 32-33; Cathy Diefendorf 118, 127; Bill Farnsworth 77; Chuck Gillies 206; Greg Hargreaves 86; Nick Harris 12-13; Dave Henderson 214; Dean Kennedy 188; Barbara Kiwak 8-9; Tim Langenderfer 45, 60, 76, 120, 121, 172, 173; Jeff Lavaty 66; Chuck Marshall 136, 196, 213;Bill Maughan; The Mazer Corporation 85; Jack Pennington 70, 128, 129; Linda Pierce 164; Jeff Preston 68, 84, 94, 163, 180; Jane Sanders 2-3, 4-5; Shannon Stirnweiss 83, 94; SuperStock 122; Christina Wald 155; Lois Woolley 48, 56, 64, 74, 90, 100, 108, 116, 126, 134, 142, 152, 160, 168, 178, 186, 194, 204, 212, 220, 229.

Photo Credits
CONTENTS
page iii Joe Brooks
SEASONAL LESSONS & CELEBRATIONS
10-11 Anatoly Sapronenkov/SuperStock ; 11 PhotoDisc; 14-15 (bkg) Bernd Obermann/Corbis; 15 (i) Creatas/PictureQuest; 15 EyeWire; 16-17 Bill Smith Studio; 18-19 Chris Alan Wilton/Getty Images; 19 Bill Smith Studio; 20-21 Archivo Iconografico, S.A./Corbis; 22-23 (bkg) Corel; 22 (i) PhotoDisc; 23 EyeWire; 24-25 Bill Wittman; 26-27 SW Productions/Getty Images; 27 PhotoDisc; 30-31 Phoebe Dunn/Stock Connection/PictureQuest; 31 PhotoDisc; 34-35 Myrleen Ferguson Cate/PhotoEdit; 34-35 (bkg) IFA/eStock Photo/PictureQuest; 35 C Squared Studios/Getty Images; 36-37 Roy Morsch/Corbis; 38-39 Morocco Flowers/Index Stock Imagery/ PictureQuest; 38-39 (bkg) Corel.

UNIT 1
40 (b) Joe Brooks Photography; 40 (c) Digital Vision; 40 (t) Ariel Skelley/Corbis; 41 (b) Areil Skelley/Corbis; 46 (br) Jim Whitmer Photography; 48 (cr) George Shelley/Corbis; 49 (all) Digital Vision; 51 (bl) Cleo Photography; 51 (cr) Gene Plaisted/The Crosiers; 52 (br) Stone/Getty Images,Inc.; 52 (tl) Myrleen Ferguson Cate/PhotoEdit; 53 (b) David Young-Wolff/PhotoEdit; 54 (c) Joseph Sohm; ChromoSohm Inc./Corbis; 57 (b) Joe Brooks Photography; 59 (br) Richard Hutchings/Hutchings Photography; 61 (cr) Sara Beth Morton/Morton Arts; 62 (br) PhotoDisc Green/Getty Images, Inc.; 64 (cr) Taxi/Getty Images, Inc.

UNIT 2
66 (c) Richard Hutchings/Hutchings Photography; 66 (t) Stone/Getty Images, Inc.; 67 (b) Stone/Getty Images, Inc.; 71 (cr) Myrleen Gerguson Cate/PhotoEdit; 72 (cr) The Crosiers/Gene Plaisted, OSC; 75 (b) Richard Hutchings/Hutchings Photography; 77 (bl) Taxi/Getty Images, Inc.; 78 (cl) Paul Markow/FPG International; 79 (cr) Stephen Epstein/PonkaWonka.com; 80 (br) Cleve Bryant/PhotoEdit; 82 (cr) Royalty-Free/Corbis; 86 (tl) Jim Daniels; 88 (cr) Tom Nebbia/Corbis; 90 (cr) The Mazer Corporation; 90 (cr) Joe Brooks Photography.

UNIT 3
92 (b) Sonny T. Senser; 92 (c) Sonny T. Senser ; 92 (t) Getty Images, Inc.; 93 (all) Getty Images, Inc.; 97 (cr) Scala/Art Resource, NY; 98 (b) Richard Hutchings/Hutchings Photography; 101 (b) Sonny T. Senser; 105 (cr) Scala/Art Resource, NY; 106 (br) Myrleen Ferguson Cate/PhotoEdit; 109 (b) Sonny T. Senser; 111 (br) Richard Hutchings/Hutchings Photography; 111 (tr) Byzantine Art; Silvio Fiore/SuperStock, Inc.; 112 (cr) Gene Plaisted/The Crosiers, OSC; 113 (cr) Marquette University Archives; 113 (tl) Catholic News Service; 114 (br) John Paul Endresst/Corbis Stock Market; 114 (cr) The Crosiers/Gene Plaisted, OSC; 116 (cr) Richard Hutchings/Hutchings Photography.

UNIT 4
118 (b) Joe Brooks Photography; 118 (t) Richard Hutchings/Hutchings Photography; 119 (all) Richard Hutchings/Hutchings Photography; 122 (cl) ©SuperStock; 123 (cr) Gene Plaisted/The Crosiers; 124 (br) Rudi Von Briel/PhotoEdit; 129 (bl) Ed McDonald Photography; 131 (cr) H. Rogers/Art Directors & TRIP Photo Library; 132 (br) The Pierpont Morgan Library/Art Resource, NY; 135 (b) Joe Brooks Photography; 137 (c) Isabelle Rozenbaum/ PhotoAlto; 138 (bkgd) Bill Wittman/WP Wittman Limited; 140 (br) Saola/Thierry Diwovie.

UNIT 5
144 (b) Steve Skjold/PhotoEdit; 144 (c) Ed McDonald Photography; 144 (t) Michael Newman/PhotoEdit; 145 (cl) Michael Newman/PhotoEdit; 146 (cl) Gene Plaisted/The Crosiers; 147 (bl) Richard Hutchings/Hutchings Photography; 147 (cr) Gene Plaisted/The Crosiers; 149 (cr) Tony Freeman/PhotoEdit; 150 (br) Richard Hutchings/Hutchings Photography; 153 (b) Ed McDonald Photography; 154 (tr) Psalm 85, copyright John August Swanson 1990; 156 (br) Jose Carillo/PhotoEdit; 157 (cr) David Young Wolff/PhotoEdit; 158 (cr) Gene Plaisted/The Crosiers; 160 (cr) Bill Wittman/WP Wittman Limited; 161 (bc) Steve Skjold/PhotoEdit; 161 (bkgd) Kai Chiang/SuperStock, Inc.; 162 (b) David Young Wolff/PhotoEdit; 165 (cr) Myrleen Ferguson Cate/PhotoEdit; 166 (br) Joe Brooks Photography; 168 (cr) Matt Meadows Photography.

UNIT 6
170 (bl) Tom Wilson/Getty Images; 170 (cl) Spencer Grant/PhotoEdit; 170 (tl) Jason Hutchings/Hutchings Photography; 171 (b) Jason Hutchings/Hutchings Photography; 173 (b) Richard Hutchings/Hutchings Photography; 174 (cl) Gene Plaisted/The Crosiers; 175 (cr) Gene Plaisted/The Crosiers; 176 (cr) David Young Wolff/PhotoEdit; 179 (cl) Spencer Grant/PhotoEdit; 181 (tr) Bob Daemmrich/Stock Boston; 182 (bc) Myrleen Ferguson Cate/PhotoEdit; 182 (bl) Bettmann/Corbis; 182 (br) Gene Plaisted/The Crosiers; 183 (cr) Bill Wittman/WP Wittman Limited; 184 (br) Tony Freeman/PhotoEdit; 187 (all) Tom Wilson/Getty Images; 189 (cr) James L. Shaffer/Shaffer Photography; 190 (b) PhotoDisc; 191 (cr) Jim Whitmer Photography; 191 (cl) James L. Shaffer/Shaffer Photography; 192 (br) Carlos Goldin/Corbis; 194 (cr) Sonny T. Senser.

UNIT 7
196 (c) Gary Buss/Getty Images; 196 (t) Bill Wittman/WP Wittman Limited; 197 (all) Bill Wittman/WP Wittman Limited ; 199 (bl) Richard Hutchings/Hutchings Photography; 199 (cr) Scala/Art Resource, NY; 200 (br) Richard Hutchings/Corbis; 201 (cr) Tony Freeman/PhotoEdit; 202 (cr) James L. Shaffer; 202 (cr) Jose Fuste Raga/Corbis; 204 (cr) Anton Vengo/SuperStock, Inc.; 205 (b) Gary Buss/Getty Images; 207 (cl) Gene Plaisted/The Crosiers; 208 (b) Harcourt Religion Publishers; 209 (tr) David Lees/Corbis; 210 (br) Digital Imaging Group/Harcourt Religion Publishers; 215 (cr) M. Angelo/Corbis; 216 (t) Dave Bartruff/Corbis ; 217 (cr) Owen Franken/Corbis; 218 (br) Pablo Corral V/Corbis.

CATHOLIC SOURCE BOOK
223 PhotoSpin; 226 Superstock; 232 Spencer Grant/PhotoEdit ; 233 Superstock; 235 Tony Freeman/PhotoEdit; 237 PhotoDisc; 238-241 (bkg) Thinkstock/Getty Images.

Acknowledgements
For permission to reprint copyrighted material, grateful acknowledgment is made to the following sources:

International Consultation on English Texts: English translation of the Glory to the Father (*Gloria Patri*), The Lord's Prayer, Holy, Holy, Holy, Lord (*Sanctus and Benedictus*), Lamb of God (*Agnus Dei*), and The Nicene Creed by International Consultation on English Texts (ICET).

Liturgy Training Publications, 1800 North Hermitage Avenue, Chicago, IL 60622, 1-800-933-1800, www.ltp.org: From "Meal Prayer for Early Spring" (Retitled: "Grace at Mealtime") in *Blessings and Prayers through the Year: A Resource for School and Parish* by Elizabeth McMahon Jeep. Text © 2004 by Archdiocese of Chicago.

Howard S. Olson: Lyrics from "Good News" by Howard S. Olson. Lyrics © 1993 by Howard S. Olson.

Twenty-Third Publications, A Division of Bayard: "Vocations" (Retitled: "Vocational Guidance") from *500 Prayers for Catholic Schools & Parish Youth Groups* by Filomena Tassi and Peter Tassi. Text copyright © 2004 by Filomena Tassi and Peter Tassi.

United States Conference of Catholic Bishops, Inc., Washington, D.C.: English translation of "Hail, Holy Queen" (Salve, Regina) and "Psalm-prayer" (Retitled: "Evening Prayer") from *Catholic Household Blessings and Prayers.* Translation copyright © 1989 by United States Catholic Conference, Inc.

World Library Publications, www.wlpmusic.com: Lyrics from "We Sing of the Saints" by Alan Hommerding. Lyrics © 1994 by World Library Publications.